THE BOOK OF

PASTA

LESLEY MACKLEY

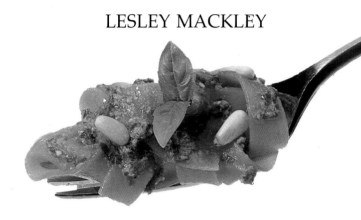

Photography by
JON STEWART

HPBooks

ANOTHER BEST-SELLING VOLUME FROM HPBOOKS

HPBOOKS
Published by The Berkley Publishing Group
200 Madison Avenue
New York, NY 10016

11

By arrangement with Salamander Books Ltd. and Merehurst Press, London.

Photographer: Jon Stewart, assisted by Alister Thorpe
Home Economist: Sarah Bush
Color separation by J. Film Process Ltd., Bangkok, Thailand
Printed in Belgium by Proost International Book Production

Library of Congress Cataloging-in-Publication Data

Mackley, Lesley.
   The book of pasta.

   Includes index.
   1. Cookery (Macaroni)   I. Title.
TX809.M17M33   1987   641.8'22   87-8721
ISBN0-89586-641-2 (pbk.)

——CONTENTS——

LESLEY MACKLEY

Lesley Mackley is a freelance home economist who creates recipes and write articles for numerous magazines. She is an avid traveler and spends some time in France each year collecting new ideas.

THE BOOK OF

—— INTRODUCTION ——

Pasta is one of the world's simplest foods, being little more than a flour and water paste, although eggs may be added for richness and color. Spinach or tomato paste can also add color and flavor. The best dried pasta is made from durum, a particularly hard variety of wheat which grows in the Midwest, and which is nutritionally superior to the wheat normally used for flour-making.

Although a simple food, pasta must also be one of the most versatile, nutritious, economical and convenient. A seemingly endless variety of dried and fresh pasta is now widely available, so that it can be an important ingredient in an enormous range of dishes, from the humblest to the most sophisticated.

Pasta is the perfect food for entertaining, but is equally suitable for serving in small quantities as there is no waste, and even an opened packet will keep well for several months. With the addition of a few items from the cupboard or refrigerator, pasta quickly can be transformed into a nutritious and satisfying meal for any number of people.

Pasta forms an ideal basis for vegetarian meals. You may prefer meat or fish, but whatever your taste, there is certain to be a pasta dish which will tempt you.

——— COOKING PASTA———

The secret of cooking pasta successfully is to use sufficient water. Allow 1 quart for every 4 ounces of pasta. Bring water to a boil; add 1 tablespoon oil and 1 tablespoon salt to each pound of pasta. Then add pasta. Long pasta such as spaghetti should be fanned out slowly into the water as it softens. Bring water back to a boil and continue boiling until the pasta is cooked. To test whether it is done, remove a piece from the water and bite into it. It should be 'al dente', or slightly firm to the bite. If pasta is to be cooked again in a baked dish, undercook slightly, as it will continue to cook in the oven. Drain pasta in a colander, shaking to remove most of the water, but leave a little water clinging to it to prevent sticking. Pour pasta on a warmed serving dish and toss with a little olive oil, butter or some of the sauce which accompanies it. If pasta is to be served in a salad or reheated in a baked dish, rinse in cold water and let drain.

The cooking times for pasta vary according to its size and shape. Follow the directions on the packet as a guideline, but keep testing during cooking time to avoid overcooking. Whole-wheat pasta takes longer and fresh pasta much less time to cook than ordinary dried pasta.

——————— TYPES OF PASTA ———————

Certain types of pasta are more suited to a particular dish than others, but pasta of a similar shape may be substituted in any recipe.

Lasagne (1)
Cooking Time: Some lasagne requires no pre-cooking and is layered straight into a dish with sauce and baked in the oven. Other lasagne must be boiled about 10 minutes before being layered with other ingredients.
Uses: Layered with meat, fish or vegetable sauces. May also be rolled around filling, like cannelloni.

Pappardelle (2)
Cooking time: 8 minutes
Uses: Traditionally served with rabbit sauce.

Tagliatelle (3) & Fettucine (4)
Cooking Time: 6 minutes
Uses: Similar to spaghetti, but particularly good with creamy sauces which adhere better than heavy sauces. May also be fried.

Spaghetti (5)
Cooking time: 12 minutes
Uses: Served simply with butter or oil, or with almost any kind of sauce.

Spaghettini (6)
Cooking time: 8 minutes
Uses: Traditionally served with fish and shellfish sauces. Also good with tomato sauce.

Vermicelli (7)
Cooking time: 5 minutes
Uses: Very thin vermicelli sold in clusters is ideal for serving with very light sauces. Long vermicelli is used in the same way as spaghetti.

Macaroni (8) & Bucatini (9)
Cooking time: 8 to 10 minutes
Uses: Often used in baked dishes, particularly those with a cheese-based sauce.

Rigatoni (10)
Cooking time: 10 minutes
Uses: Generally used in baked dishes. The ridges help the sauce to cling to the pasta. It may also be stuffed.

Penne (11)
Cooking time: 10 minutes
Uses: Served with meat sauces which catch in the hollows.

Cannelloni (12)
Cooking time: Most cannelloni tubes require no pre-cooking and are stuffed directly before baking. If they are to be fried, they should be boiled first 7 to 10 minutes.
Uses: Filled cannelloni may be baked in the oven in a sauce or topped with butter and grated cheese, and may also be deep-fried until crisp.

Conchiglie (13)
Cooking time: Large shells take about 15 minutes to cook and smaller ones about 10 minutes.
Uses: Large shells may be stuffed, and their shape makes a fish filling particularly appropriate. Smaller shells are used in casseroles and soup, and served cold in salads.

Fiochetti (bows) (14) & Farfalle (butterflies) (15)
Cooking time: 10 minutes
Uses: Ideal for serving with meat or vegetable sauces, which become trapped in the folds.

Fusilli (16) & Tortiglioni (spirals) (17)
Cooking time: 10 minutes
Uses: Served with substantial meat sauces, which are trapped in the twists. Also good in salads.

Lumache (18)
Cooking time: 10 minutes
Uses: Similar to conchiglie.

Rotini (wheels) (19) & Anelli (20)
Cooking time: 8 minutes
Uses: Added to savory bakes and salads.

Pastina (anellini, ditalini, stellini) (21)
Cooking time: 8 minutes
Uses: Most often added to soups, but may be used in many other dishes.

Egg Noodles (22)
Cooking time: 4 to 5 minutes
Uses: Flat noodles are often served in soups. Round ones are served in sauces, and are best for stir-frying. Also served as an accompaniment instead of rice.

Rice Noodles (23)
Cooking time: Simply soak in hot water 10 to 15 minutes.
Uses: Served in spicy sauces, soups and stir-fry dishes.

Transparent (Cellophane) Noodles (24)
Cooking time: Soak in hot water 5 minutes.
Uses: Added to soup or deep-fried as a garnish.

—— MAKING FRESH PASTA ——

BASIC PASTA DOUGH
2 eggs
1-1/2 cups bread flour
Pinch salt

Any quantity of pasta may be made by using the proportions of 1 egg to 3/4 cup flour, but the most convenient quantity to handle, particularly for a beginner, is a 2- to 3-egg mixture. Larger amounts should be mixed and rolled in batches.

Beat eggs in a large bowl. Sift flour and salt over eggs. Mix together with a fork, then press into a ball with the hands. It should be firm but pliable, and not sticky. Add more flour if too moist.

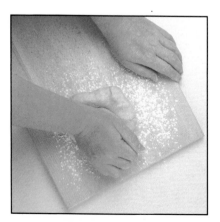

Turn the dough onto a lightly floured surface, and knead firmly 5 to 10 minutes or until smooth. Wrap in a damp towel and let rest 30 minutes at room temperature.

Variations

PASTA VERDI:
Cook 4 ounces spinach. Drain, squeeze out as much moisture as possible and chop very fine. Add spinach to the eggs and flour, adding extra flour if necessary.

TOMATO PASTA:
Add 1 tablespoon tomato paste to the eggs and flour.

HERB PASTA:
Add 1 tablespoon of a single fresh herb, such as parsley, or mixed fresh herbs, to the eggs and flour.

WHOLE-WHEAT PASTA:
Use whole-wheat flour in place of white flour or, for a lighter texture, a mixture of whole-wheat and white flour.

—ROLLING PASTA BY HAND—

When rolling pasta by hand, you will need a long rolling pin and a large, clear work surface. It is essential to work quickly, or the pasta will dry out and crack. Roll away from you, and keep lifting the sheet of pasta on the rolling pin, turning it 45 degrees as you roll. Lift the far edge on the rolling pin, and push it away from you to stretch the dough.

As the sheet of pasta becomes larger, allow it to hang over the edge of the table to increase the stretch. Eventually, the sheet of pasta should look smooth and suede-like in texture, and it should be so thin that you can read newsprint through it. Unless you are an expert, you will not be able to roll the pasta as thin by hand as with a machine. Therefore you will probably find that you need a slightly larger quantity of pasta than that given in a recipe.

If you are making lasagne or filled pasta, such as ravioli or tortellini, the pasta should be used immediately. Otherwise, it should be spread on a towel and left to dry 30 minutes. Turn it over after 15 minutes. Let dry long enough to prevent it sticking, but not so much that it becomes brittle. The dough is then ready for cutting into shapes.

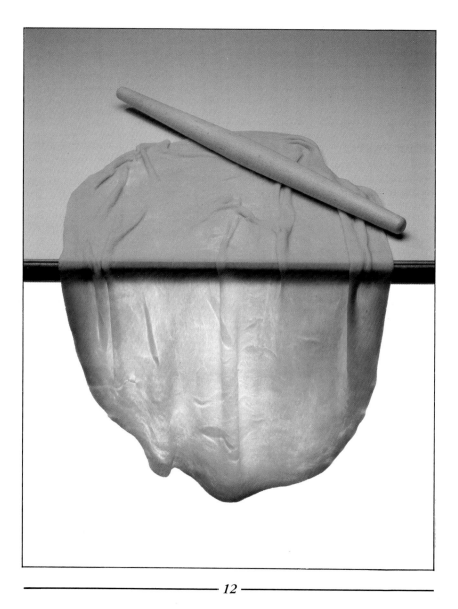

— CUTTING PASTA SHAPES —

TAGLIATELLE:

Loosely roll up pasta dough in a cylinder. Using a sharp knife, cut cylinder in even widths. Shake out coils in loose nests. These may be cooked immediately or left to dry for several days before being stored.

LASAGNE & CANNELLONI:

Using a sharp knife or serrated pasta-cutting wheel, cut lasagne sheets to whatever size will best fit your dish. For most purposes, sheets measuring 5" x 4" are the most convenient. For cannelloni, cut pasta as for lasagne. The sheets can then be cooked and rolled around a stuffing before baking in oven.

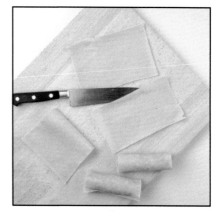

PAPPARDELLE & FARFALLE:

For pappardelle, using a serrated pasta-cutting wheel, cut pasta in strips 12" long and 3/4" wide. For farfalle, cut pasta sheet in 2" squares with pasta-cutting wheel. Pinch each square together in middle to produce a butterfly effect.

Note: Cut pasta trimmings in pretty shapes with a biscuit or aspic cutter and use for garnishing soups.

—————— PASTA MACHINES ——————

Electric machines are available which mix the dough and then extrude it through the selected cutter, but unless you intend to make large quantitites of pasta on a regular basis, they are not necessary.

The most useful machine is a hand cranking one which rolls the pasta into sheets and has cutters of different widths through which the sheets can be passed. One machine has an attachment for mixing the pasta, but this is not an essential refinement, particularly if you have a food processor. To mix pasta dough in a food processor, process the eggs 30 seconds, then add the sifted flour and salt and process until the mixture forms a ball.

By fitting cutters of various sizes onto your pasta rolling machine, it is possible to cut spaghetti or noodles in several different widths. Do not cut spaghetti into long sheets of pasta which tend to stick together. Place a towel over the back of a chair and spread the spaghetti or noodles out to dry about 30 minutes.

-ROLLING PASTA IN A MACHINE-

Divide the dough into as many pieces as the number of eggs used. Set the rollers of the machine to the widest setting. Flatten the pieces of dough and roll each through in turn.

Fold each piece in thirds, crosswise, and feed through again. Do this about eight times, or until the sheet of pasta is smooth and silky. Set the rollers one notch closer together and feed the pasta through once on each setting.

Cut the sheets of pasta in half if they become too long to hand easily. A final rolling on the narrowest but one setting should produce pasta of the correct thickness for most purposes.

RAVIOLI:

When making ravioli, prepare the filling first and set aside. Then make the dough, see page 10, and roll into strips. Lay the strips out on a towel or floured surface and keep those you are not working on covered with a damp cloth.

Place small amounts (1/2 teaspoon) of filling at 1-1/2-inch intervals over sheet of pasta and lay a second sheet over the top.

Press down firmly between the mounds of pasta, and cut between the mounds with a pastry wheel. Spread the ravioli out on a towel to dry about 30 minutes, turning over after 15 minutes. Take care to keep separate, or they will stick together. Round ravioli, or agnolotti, is made by cutting circles from the filled sheets of pasta.

ROUND RAVIOLI:

Cut circles from the filled sheets of pasta using a sharp knife, serrated pasta-cutting wheel or a special round pasta-cutting stamp.

HALF MOON RAVIOLI:

Cut circles about 2" in diameter. Place a pea-sized amount of filling in the middle. Fold over 1 side of the circle and press edges firmly together. Leave to dry as for ravioli.

TORTELLINI:

Cut circles about 2 inches in diameter. Place a pea-sized amount of filling slightly to 1 side of the middle. Fold over 1 side of the circle so that it falls just short of the other side and press the edges firmly together. Curve the semi-circle round and pinch the edges together. Let dry in the same way as ravioli.

CAPPELLETTI:

Cut 2-inch squares of pasta. Put a small amount of filling in the center of each square. Fold in half diagonally to form a triangle, leaving a slight overlap between the edges. Press firmly to seal. Wrap the long side of the triangle around a finger until the 2 ends overlap. Press the ends firmly together with the points of the triangle upright. Let dry in the same way as ravioli.

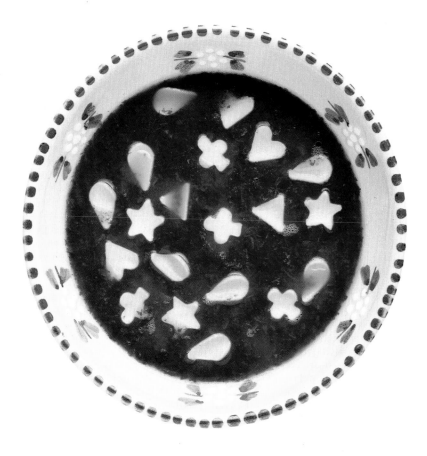

Spinach Soup

**1 quart Chicken Stock, see page 27
1/2 cup annelini (2 oz.)
1 (10-oz.) pkg. frozen chopped
  spinach, thawed
2 egg yolks, beaten
Salt and pepper**

Bring stock to a boil in a medium-size saucepan. Add annelini and spinach. Cook 10 minutes, stirring occasionally, or until pasta is just tender to the bite. Beat a little hot soup into egg yolks. Stir egg mixture into soup; heat until hot. Do not allow soup to boil. Season to taste. Serve at once. Makes 4 to 6 servings.

Variation
Garnish soup with pasta shapes cut from fresh pasta, see page 13.

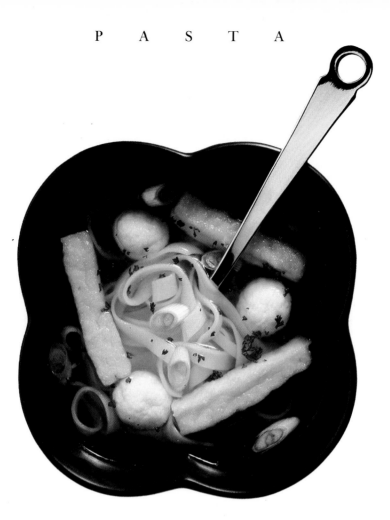

Penang Fish Soup

1 cup fish trimmings (bones, skins,
  heads)
1 quart salted water
1 lb. skinned white fish fillets, such as
  cod or haddock
1 teaspoon chopped fresh parsley
Salt and pepper
Oil for deep-frying
2 oz. wide rice noodles or rice sticks
4 green onions, finely chopped
Additional chopped fresh parsley

Put fish trimmings and water into a medium-size saucepan. Bring to a boil; reduce heat. Cover pan; simmer 20 minutes. In a blender or food processor, process fish until it forms a smooth paste. Add 1 teaspoon chopped parsley. Season with salt and pepper. Roll 1/2 of paste in small balls 1/2 inch in diameter. Flatten out remaining paste in a rectangular cake 2 inches wide. Cut in strips. Deep-fry strips until crisp and golden. Drain on paper towels. Keep hot. Strain fish broth through a fine sieve into a 2-quart saucepan. Bring back to a boil. Add fishballs. Cook gently 5 minutes. Meanwhile, in a large pan of boiling salted water, cook noodles until just tender to the bite. Drain; divide among 4 heated bowls. Divide fishballs among bowls. Pour in broth. Arrange fried fish strips on top. Garnish with green onions and additional chopped parsley. Makes 4 servings.

Minestrone Soup

3 tablespoons olive oil
4 (1-oz.) thin slices ham, cut into
  matchsticks
1 onion, chopped
2 carrots, chopped
2 celery stalks, chopped
8 oz. white cabbage, coarsely
  shredded (4 cups)
1 medium-size zucchini, diced (2 cups)
4 oz. green beans, cut into 1-inch
  lengths
6 cups Chicken Stock, see page 27
1 (15-oz.) can tomatoes
Salt and pepper
3/4 cup macaroni (4 oz.)
1 tablespoon chopped fresh parsley
Freshly shredded Parmesan cheese

In a large saucepan, heat olive oil.
Add ham, onion, carrots and celery.
Cook gently until beginning to soften. Add cabbage, zucchini, beans, stock, tomatoes with juice, salt and pepper. Bring to a boil; reduce heat. Cover; simmer about 2 hours. Add macaroni. Cook 10 to 15 minutes or until macaroni is just tender to the bite. Add parsley. Serve with Parmesan cheese. Makes 6 to 8 servings.

Variation:
Vary the vegetables according to taste and availability. Pesto, see page 43, may be stirred in before serving.

White Onion Soup

1/4 cup butter
3 medium-size onions, finely
   sliced (1-1/2 cups)
1 tablespoon all-purpose flour
1-1/4 cups boiling water
3-3/4 cups milk
2 oz. straight vermicelli, broken into
   1/2-inch pieces
Salt and pepper
Fresh parsley, if desired
12 to 18 bacon rolls, if desired

In a medium-size saucepan, melt butter. Add onions. Cook gently until
soft. Stir in flour; cook until bubbly.
Gradually stir in hot water. Cook,
stirring, until sauce is smooth and
thickened. Stir in milk. Bring to a
boil. Add vermicelli, salt and pepper.
Cover pan. Cook, stirring frequently,
until vermicelli is just tender to the
bite. Place parsley and bacon rolls on
wooden picks and garnish soup, if
desired. Makes 4 to 6 servings.

Tomato & Pasta Soup

8 medium-size tomatoes
1/4 cup butter
1 medium-size onion, finely chopped
  (1/2 cup)
1/3 cup ditalini or elbow macaroni
  (2 oz.)
1 quart Chicken Stock, see page 27
Pinch of saffron
Pinch of chili powder
Salt
Fresh parsley, if desired

Put tomatoes into a bowl. Cover with boiling water 1 minute. Drain. Cover with cold water 1 minute. Drain. Remove and discard skins and chop tomatoes. In a large saucepan, melt butter. Add onion. Cook until beginning to soften. Add ditalini; cook, stirring, 2 minutes. Add tomatoes. Add stock and saffron. Bring to a boil; reduce heat. Cover; simmer until ditalini is just tender to the bite. Stir in chili powder and salt to taste. Garnish with parsley, if desired. Makes 4 servings.

Light Vegetable Soup

3-3/4 cups vegetable stock, made from vegetable trimmings or bouillon cube
2 carrots
2 celery stalks, thinly sliced
1-1/2 cups thinly sliced button mushrooms (3 oz.)
3/4 cup frozen peas (2 oz.)
2 tablespoons small pasta shells (1 oz.)
Salt and pepper
1 tablespoon chopped fresh parsley

Bring stock to a boil in a medium-size saucepan. With the pointed end of a potato peeler, cut grooves down carrots. Cut into thin slices. Add to stock with celery, mushrooms, peas and pasta. Bring to a boil; reduce heat. Cover pan; simmer about 15 minutes, or until pasta and vegetables are just tender to the bite. Season with salt and pepper and sprinkle .with parsley. Makes 4 servings.

Bean & Pasta Soup

2 tablespoons olive oil
1 medium-size onion, finely chopped
1 garlic clove, crushed
2 carrots, finely chopped
2 celery stalks, finely chopped
1-1/2 quarts Chicken Stock, see
  page 27
Salt and pepper
1-1/2 cups pasta shells (3 oz.)
1 (15-oz.) can pinto beans
Celery leaves, if desired

Heat oil in a medium-size saucepan over medium heat. Add onion, garlic, carrots and celery; cook until soft. Add stock, salt and pepper. Bring to a boil. Cover; simmer 20 minutes. Add pasta; cook 10 minutes more or until pasta is just tender to the bite. Drain beans. Rinse in cold water. Sieve, or process 1/2 of beans in a blender or food processor. Add puréed and whole beans to soup. Stir well. Cook 2 more minutes. Garnish with celery, if desired. Makes 6 to 8 servings.

Chicken Noodle Soup

1 quart Chicken Stock, see page 27
1 carrot, cut into matchsticks
1 leek, thinly sliced
2 cups chopped cooked chicken
3 oz. round egg noodles
Salt and pepper
Fresh cilantro, if desired

Bring stock to a boil in a medium-size saucepan. Add carrot and leek. Cover pan; simmer about 5 minutes or until carrot and leek are just tender to the bite. Stir in chicken, egg noodles, salt and pepper. Cook 5 to 10 minutes or until noodles are just tender to the bite. Garnish with cilantro, if desired, and serve at once in individual bowls. Makes 4 servings.

Avgolemono Soup

1 quart Chicken Stock, see page 27
1/3 cup pastina (1-1/2 oz.)
Salt and pepper
2 eggs
Juice of 1 lemon
Lemon slices, if desired
Fresh herbs, if desired

Bring stock to a boil in a small saucepan. Add pastina; season with salt
and pepper. Cook 5 minutes or until
pastina is just tender to the bite. In a
medium-size bowl, beat eggs. Add
lemon juice; beat to mix thoroughly.
Whisk a ladleful of hot stock into
eggs. Pour egg mixture into stock in
saucepan. Over a low heat, whisk
constantly 3 to 4 minutes or until
soup thickens slightly. Garnish with
lemon and herbs, if desired. Makes 4
servings.

Note: The soup must not boil or the
eggs will scramble.

Won-Ton Soup

2 quarts Chicken Stock, see below
24 filled won-tons, see page 97
Chinese cabbage leaves
Carrot strips
1 green onion, finely chopped

Chicken Stock:
1 (3-1/2-lb.) broiler-fryer chicken with
  giblets
2 quarts water
1 medium-size onion
1 leek
1 celery stalk
1 small bunch fresh parsley
Salt and pepper

Bring stock to a boil in a 4-quart saucepan. Drop won-tons, cabbage leaves and carrots into stock. Boil rapidly 2 to 3 minutes or until won-tons are tender but firm. Garnish with green onion and serve in individual bowls. Makes 4 to 6 servings.

To make stock: Put chicken, giblets, water and onion into a large saucepan. Tie together leek, celery and parsley in cheesecloth. Add to pan with salt and pepper. Bring to a boil; reduce heat. Simmer, covered, 2 hours. Occasionally remove any scum from the surface. Strain stock; adjust seasoning. When cool, refrigerate until following day. Remove fat from surface of stock. Makes about 2 quarts.

Note: Meat from cooked chicken can be used in other dishes. Remaining stock will keep 2 to 3 days in the refrigerator, or may be stored in the freezer.

- Smoked Salmon & Avocado Roll -

1 bunch watercress
3 green onions, very finely chopped
1 tablespoon olive oil
1 teaspoon prepared horseradish
Salt and pepper
1 avocado
Juice of 1/2 lemon
3 cooked green lasagne noodles
3 oz. smoked salmon, thinly sliced
1/4 cup mayonnaise
1/4 cup crème fraîche
1 tablespoon chopped fresh dill weed
Milk as needed
Lemon peel strips, if desired
Fresh dill, if desired

In a saucepan of boiling water, blanch watercress 10 seconds. Drain; refresh in a bowl of cold water. Squeeze gently in a cloth to dry. Chop fine. In a small bowl, mix together watercress, green onions, olive oil, horseradish, salt and pepper. Halve and pit avocado; peel. Cut in lengthwise slices. Toss avocado in lemon juice. Spread a little watercress mixture over each sheet of lasagne. Lay a slice of smoked salmon on each sheet. Arrange avocado slices in a line down the length of the middle of each sheet. Starting with a long side of pasta, roll up jelly-roll fashion. Wrap each roll in plastic wrap. Chill 2 hours. In a bowl, mix together mayonnaise, crème fraîche, dill weed, salt and pepper. Add a little milk, if necessary, to make a pouring consistency. Cut each roll diagonally in slices 3/4-inch wide. Garnish with lemon peel strips and dill, if desired. Serve with dill sauce. Makes 4 to 6 first course servings.

Seafood Pasta Salad

12 oz. monkfish, skinned
1/4 cup dry white wine
3 oz. smoked salmon trout
4 oz. cooked shrimp, peeled, deveined
4 cups pasta verti spirals (8 oz.),
   cooked
1/4 teaspoon dried dill weed
Lemon slices, if desired
Fresh dill, if desired

Dressing:
Salt and pepper
1/2 teaspoon dry mustard
1 garlic clove, crushed
1 tablespoon lemon juice
1/3 cup olive oil

Cut monkfish in cubes; put into a small saucepan with wine and enough water to cover. Cook for a few minutes until fish is tender. Drain; let cool. Cut trout in strips. In a large bowl, combine monkfish, trout, shrimp, pasta and dill weed. Make Dressing. Pour Dressing over pasta mixture. Mix thoroughly. Garnish with lemon slices and dill, if desired. Makes 4 servings.

To make Dressing: In a small bowl, mix together salt, pepper, mustard, garlic and lemon juice. Gradually stir in olive oil.

Three-Colored Pasta Salad

6 green onions
1 small red bell pepper, diced
1 small green bell pepper, diced
1 recipe Dressing, see page 29
4 cups red, green and white pasta
shells (8 oz.)

Chop green onions until fine. In a
bowl, combine green onions and bell
peppers with Dressing. In a large
saucepan of boiling salted water,
cook pasta until just tender to the
bite. Drain; rinse in cold water. Drain
thoroughly. In a large bowl, mix
together Dressing and pasta. Makes 4
to 6 servings.

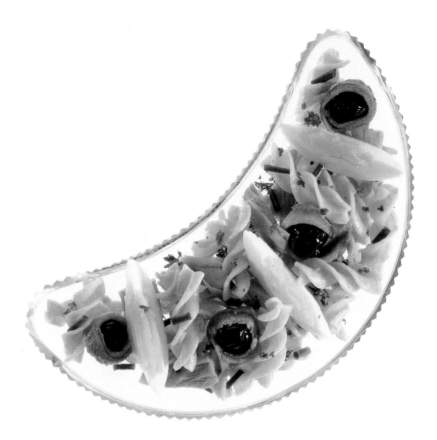

Pasta Niçoise

4 cups whole-wheat pasta
  spirals (8 oz.)
6 canned anchovies, drained
6 pitted black olives, sliced
1 (6-oz.) can tuna, drained, flaked
1 tablespoon chopped fresh parsley
1 tablespoon chopped chives
1 hard-boiled egg, cut in wedges

Dressing:
Salt and pepper
1 teaspoon Dijon-style mustard
1 garlic clove, crushed
1 tablespoon white wine vinegar
1/3 cup olive oil

In a large saucepan of boiling salted water, cook pasta until just tender to the bite. Drain; rinse in cold water. Drain thoroughly. Cut each anchovy in half lengthwise. Wrap anchovy fillets around olives. Drain tuna. In a large bowl, combine cooked pasta, tuna, parsley and chives. Make Dressing. Pour Dressing over pasta mixture. Mix thoroughly. Arrange olives and egg over pasta mixture. Makes 4 servings.

To make Dressing: In a small bowl, mix together salt, pepper, mustard, garlic, vinegar and oil.

Tarragon Chicken Salad

4 cups pasta verdi shells (8 oz.)
1 (3-lb.) broiler-fryer chicken, cooked
8 oz. seedless grapes
1 tablespoon chopped fresh tarragon
1/4 cup mayonnaise
1/4 cup crème fraîche
Salt and pepper
Fresh Italian parsley, if desired

In a large saucepan of boiling salted water, cook pasta until just tender to the bite. Drain; rinse in cold water. Drain thoroughly. Remove meat from chicken; cut in pieces. In a large bowl, mix cooked pasta, chicken pieces, grapes and tarragon. In a small bowl, mix together mayonnaise and crème fraîche. Season with salt and pepper. Pour over chicken; mix thoroughly. Garnish with parsley, if desired, and serve at room temperature. Makes 6 servings.

— Avocado & Orange Pasta Salad –

4 cups pasta bows (8 oz.)
1 large avocado
Grated peel and juice of 1/2 orange
Salt and pepper
Orange slices
Orange peel, if desired
Smoked salmon cornets, if desired
Fresh dill, if desired

In a large saucepan of boiling salted water, cook pasta until just tender to the bite. Drain; rinse in cold water. Drain thoroughly. Halve avocado; remove pit. Scoop out pulp, taking care to scrape all dark green flesh from skin. Put avocado, grated orange peel and juice, salt and pepper into a blender or food processor. Purée until smooth. In a large bowl, combine avocado purée and pasta. Mix until pasta is coated with avocado purée. Top with orange slices. Garnish with orange peel, salmon coronets and dill, if desired. Makes 6 servings as an accompaniment.

Note: Serve soon after making or avocado will discolor.

Greek Pasta Salad

3/4 cup taramosalata (4 oz.)
3/4 cup plain yogurt
Salt and pepper
8 oz. green noodles, cooked, drained
1/2 cup feta cheese (2 oz.)
1/2 cup ripe olives
Lemon wedges, if desired

In a large bowl, mix together taramosalata, yogurt, salt and pepper.
Add green noodles to taramosalata
mixture. Mix gently until pasta is well
coated with dressing. Cut feta cheese
into small dice. Stir cheese and olives
into noodles. Garnish with lemon
wedges, if desired. Makes 4 servings.

- Creamy Mushroom & Pea Sauce -

1/3 cup butter
2 cups sliced mushrooms (4 oz.)
2/3 cup crème fraîche
2 egg yolks
1/2 cup grated Parmesan
    cheese (1-1/2 oz.)
Salt, pepper and nutmeg
1/2 (10-oz.) pkg. frozen
    green peas
Hot cooked pasta
Fresh mint, if desired

In a medium-size skillet, melt 2 table-spoons of butter. Add mushrooms. Cook gently until tender. Set aside. In a medium-size bowl, beat together crème fraîche, egg yolks, Parmesan cheese, salt, pepper and nutmeg. In a medium-size saucepan, melt remaining butter. Stir in crème fraîche mixture. Add peas. Cook over very low heat, stirring, until mixture is heated through and begins to thicken slightly. Stir in cooked mushrooms. Serve over pasta at once and garnish with mint, if desired. Makes 4 servings.

— Mascarpone & Walnut Sauce —

1 tablespoon butter
1 cup mascarpone (8 oz.)
Milk as needed
3/4 cup walnuts, coarsely
  chopped (3 oz.)
1/4 cup shredded Parmesan
  cheese (3/4 oz.)

In a small saucepan, melt butter.
Gradually stir in mascarpone. Cook
over low heat, stirring, until sauce is
smooth. If necessary, add a little milk
to give a smooth, creamy consistency.
Stir in walnuts and Parmesan cheese.
Season with salt and pepper and
serve at once. Makes 4 servings.

Note: Serve over cooked spaghetti or
tagliatelle.

Chicken Liver Sauce

2 tablespoons butter
4 bacon slices, chopped
1 medium-size onion, finely
   chopped (1/2 cup)
1 garlic clove, crushed
12 oz. chicken livers,
   chopped (1-1/2 cups)
2 teaspoons all-purpose flour
3/4 cup Chicken Stock, see page 27
1 teaspoon tomato paste
Salt and pepper
1 teaspoon chopped fresh marjoram
1/4 cup dairy sour cream
Cooked rigatoni
Fresh marjoram, if desired

In a small saucepan, melt butter. Add
bacon, onion and garlic. Cook over
medium heat until onion is soft. Stir
in chicken livers. Cook, stirring, until
livers are no longer pink. Stir in flour.
Gradually stir in stock. Add tomato
paste, salt, pepper and chopped marjoram. Bring to a boil; reduce heat.
Cover pan; simmer 10 minutes. Stir
in sour cream and serve with rigatoni.
Garnish with marjoram, if desired.
Makes about 3 cups sauce.

Rabbit Sauce

1 (about 1-lb.) saddle of rabbit
1 cup dry red wine
1 onion, sliced
1 celery stalk, sliced
1 bay leaf
2 black peppercorns
2 tablespoons vegetable oil
6 bacon slices, chopped
1 onion, finely chopped
1 carrot, finely chopped
2 teaspoons all-purpose flour
2/3 cup Chicken Stock, see page 27
Salt, pepper and nutmeg

Put rabbit in a medium-size bowl; cover with wine. Add sliced onion, celery, bay leaf and peppercorns.

Cover bowl. Let marinate, in the refrigerator, 1 to 2 days. In a medium-size saucepan, heat oil. Add bacon, chopped onion and carrot. Cook gently until onion is soft. Remove rabbit from marinade; pat dry. Add to pan; brown all over. Stir in flour. Strain marinade; gradually add to pan with stock. Cover pan; cook over low heat 1-1/2 hours, or until rabbit is very tender. Remove rabbit from pan. Cut meat from bones. Chop into small pieces; return to pan. Makes 4 servings.

Note: This sauce is traditionally served with pappardelle, a wide ribbon pasta.

Shellfish Sauce

1/3 cup olive oil
1 lb. fresh mussels in shells, cleaned
1 garlic clove, crushed
2 shallots, finely chopped
2/3 cup dry white wine
Salt and pepper
1 (8-oz.) can clams, drained
2 tablespoons chopped fresh parsley

In a deep skillet with a cover, heat 3 tablespoons of olive oil. Add mussels. Cover pan; cook over medium heat about 4 minutes until all mussels are open. Discard mussels that do not open. Heat remaining oil in a medium-size saucepan. Add garlic and shallots. Cook until shallots are soft. Drain mussels. Strain cooking liquid; add to shallots with white wine. Bring to a boil. Boil gently, uncovered, until reduced slightly. Season with salt and pepper. Remove most mussels from shells, leaving a few for garnishing. Add mussels and clams to cooking juice. Sprinkle parsley over sauce. Serve at once. Makes 4 servings.

Carbonara Sauce

8 bacon slices
2 tablespoons butter
4 large eggs
1/2 cup grated Parmesan
cheese (1-1/2 oz.)
2 tablespoons half and half
Salt and pepper
1 tablespoon chopped fresh chives
Cooked spaghetti or tagliatelle

Finely chop bacon. In a medium-size saucepan, melt butter over medium heat. Add bacon. Fry, stirring occasionally, until crisp. In a medium-size bowl, beat together eggs, Parmesan cheese, half and half, salt and pepper. Add to bacon. Cook over medium heat, stirring, until eggs begin to thicken. Stir in chives. Pour sauce over hot spaghetti or tagliatelle. Serve at once. Makes 4 servings.

— Shrimp & Garlic Butter Sauce —

2 tablespoons olive oil
1/3 cup butter
2 garlic cloves, finely chopped
8 oz. shrimp, cooked, peeled, deveined
Salt and pepper
2 tablespoons chopped fresh chives

In a small saucepan, heat oil and butter over medium heat until butter is melted. Add garlic. Cook, stirring occasionally, 2 to 3 minutes. Stir in shrimp. Cook until heated through. Season with salt and pepper. Sprinkle with chives. Makes 4 servings.

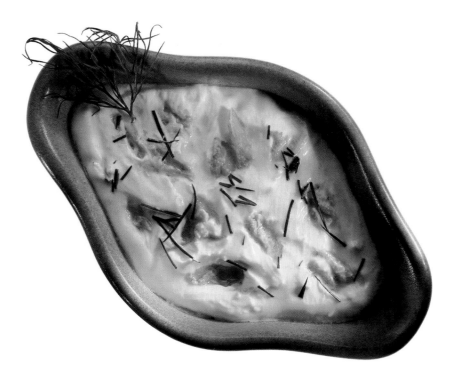

—— Salmon & Cream Sauce ——

2 tablespoons butter
1 pint half and half (2 cups)
1/4 cup grated Parmesan
  cheese (3/4 oz.)
2 cups cooked flaked salmon
1 tablespoon chopped fresh dill
Salt, pepper and nutmeg
Fresh dill, if desired

In a medium-size saucepan, heat butter and half and half over low heat.
Bring to just below boiling point. Reduce heat. Simmer gently about 10
minutes or until thickened and slightly reduced. Add Parmesan cheese.
Stir in salmon, chopped dill, salt, pepper and nutmeg. Garnish with dill, if
desired. Makes 4 servings.

Pesto

1/2 cup fresh basil leaves
1/2 cup pine nuts
2 garlic cloves
Salt
1/2 cup grated Parmesan
  cheese (1-1/2 oz.)
1/2 cup olive oil
Cooked pasta

Put basil leaves, pine nuts, garlic and salt in a blender or food processor. Process until mixture forms a paste. Add Parmesan cheese to basil mixture; process until well blended. Add oil, a little at a time; process until sauce has a creamy consistency. Makes 4 to 6 servings.

Variation
When fresh basil leaves are unavailable, a version of pesto may be made with fresh parsley. Use walnuts instead of pine nuts.

Note: Pesto is used as a sauce for pasta, and is also added to dishes such as minestrone soup to give added flavor.

Lemon & Green Peppercorn Sauce

2 tablespoons butter
2/3 cup half and half
1 to 2 teaspoons green
   peppercorns, drained
Grated peel of 1 lemon
Salt

In a small saucepan, melt butter. Stir in half and half. Lightly crush peppercorns with the back of a spoon. Add to sauce. Stir in lemon peel and salt. Cook over low heat, without boiling, until slightly thickened. Makes 4 servings.

Note: This sauce is ideal for serving with fine capellini.

Tomato Sauce

1 lb. tomatoes (3 to 4 medium-size)
4 teaspoons olive oil
1 onion, finely chopped
1 garlic clove, crushed
1 tablespoon tomato paste
1/2 teaspoon sugar
1 tablespoon chopped fresh basil
Salt and pepper
Fresh basil, if desired

Put tomatoes in a medium-size bowl. Add boiling water to cover. Blanch 1 minute; drain. Peel; chop coarsely. In a medium-size saucepan, heat oil over medium heat. Add onion and garlic. Cook until soft. Stir in chopped tomatoes, tomato paste, sugar, chopped basil, salt and pepper. Cover pan; reduce heat to low and cook about 30 minutes or until thickened. If a thicker sauce is required, heat, uncovered, a few more minutes. Garnish with basil, if desired. Makes 4 servings.

Note: For a smooth sauce, process in a blender or food processor.

—— Spaghetti with Meatballs ——

1 bread slice, crusts removed
Water
1 onion, very finely chopped
1 garlic clove, crushed
1 lb. lean ground beef
1 tablespoon chopped fresh parsley
Salt and pepper
1 tablespoon vegetable oil
1 recipe Tomato Sauce, see page 45
12 oz. spaghetti
1/2 cup grated Parmesan
   cheese (1-1/2 oz.)
Fresh basil, if desired

Soak bread in a little water. Squeeze dry and crumble into a bowl. Add onion, garlic, ground beef, parsley, salt and pepper. Mix well. Shape in 1-inch balls. Heat oil in a 10-inch skillet over medium heat. Add meatballs. Cook about 10 minutes or until browned all over. Drain off excess fat. Add Tomato Sauce. Cook until heated through. Cook spaghetti, see pages 7-8. Drain well; pour into a heated serving dish. Add meatballs and sauce. Sprinkle with Parmesan cheese. Garnish with basil, if desired, and serve. Makes 4 servings.

— Ricotta, Leek & Ham Sauce —

2 tablespoons butter
2 leeks, thinly sliced
1 garlic clove, crushed
4 (1-oz.) thin ham slices
8 oz. ricotta cheese (2 cups)
2/3 cup dairy sour cream
Milk
Pepper
Cooked tagliatelle

In a medium-size saucepan over medium heat, melt butter; add leeks and garlic. Cook until leeks are soft. Cut ham into small squares. Stir into leeks. Cook a few minutes. In a medium-size bowl, mix together ricotta and sour cream. Add a little milk, if necessary, to make a smooth creamy sauce. Season with pepper. Add to pan with leeks and ham. Reduce heat to low; cook until sauce is heated through. Serve at once with tagliatelle. Makes 4 servings.

Béchamel Sauce

1-1/4 cups milk
1/2 bay leaf
1/4 cup butter
1/4 cup all-purpose flour
Salt and pepper

In a small saucepan, heat milk and bay leaf over low heat to just below boiling point. Remove from heat. Remove and discard bay leaf. In a small saucepan, melt butter over medium heat. Stir in flour, cook 2 minutes, stirring constantly. Remove from heat. Gradually stir in hot milk. Return pan to heat. Stir until thick and smooth. Reduce heat to low and cook 10 minutes stirring occasionally. Season with salt and pepper. If sauce is not to be used immediately, cover surface closely with plastic wrap. Makes 4 servings.

Variation
Ham & Mushroom Sauce
6 oz. fresh mushrooms, sliced
  (about 2-1/2 cups)
3 tablespoons dry apple cider
4 oz. ham, cut in shreds (about 1 cup)
Grated nutmeg
Béchamel Sauce made with 1-3/4 cups
  milk, 3 tablespoons each butter and
  all-purpose flour
Hot cooked pasta

In a small saucepan, combine mushrooms with cider. Cover pan. Cook over low heat 5 minutes. Add mushrooms, cooking liquid, ham and nutmeg to Béchamel Sauce. Serve with pasta.

Green & Blue Sauce

8 oz. broccoli
6 oz. Gorgonzola cheese
1/2 cup mascarpone (3-1/2 oz.)
1 cup plain yogurt
Pepper
Hot cooked Pasta Verdi, see pages
  10-11

Wash and trim broccoli, discarding stalks. Cut in small flowerets. Cook in boiling salted water 2 to 3 minutes or until crisp-tender. Drain thoroughly. Roughly chop cheese. Put cheese and mascarpone in a small saucepan. Stir over low heat until cheese has melted. Add broccoli and yogurt to cheese sauce. Heat gently, stirring occasionally, 2 minutes. Pour over pasta. Makes 4 servings.

Mediterranean Sauce

1 medium-size eggplant
Salt
1/4 cup olive oil
1 onion, chopped
1 garlic clove, crushed
1 small green bell pepper
1 small red bell pepper
1 small yellow bell pepper
4 medium-size tomatoes, peeled,
    coarsely chopped
Salt and pepper
1/2 teaspoon dried leaf oregano
Hot cooked spaghetti

Cut eggplant in 3/4-inch strips. Put into a colander; sprinkle with salt. Let stand 1 hour. Pat dry with paper towels. In a deep 12-inch skillet with a cover, heat oil. Add onion and garlic. Cook over low heat until soft. Add eggplant. Cook, stirring occasionally, 5 minutes. Cut peppers in 3/4-inch strips. Add to skillet; cook 5 minutes. Stir in tomatoes, salt, pepper and oregano. Cover pan and cook gently 20 minutes. Serve with spaghetti. Makes 4 servings.

Bolognese Sauce

2 tablespoons vegetable oil
2 slices bacon, chopped
1 onion, finely chopped
1 carrot, finely chopped
1 celery stalk, finely chopped
1 garlic clove, crushed
8 oz. lean ground beef
4 oz. chicken livers, chopped (1/2 cup)
2 tablespoons tomato paste
1/2 cup dry white wine
1/2 cup beef stock
Salt, pepper and nutmeg
Hot cooked spaghetti
Celery leaves, if desired

In a large saucepan, heat oil over medium heat. Add bacon; cook until lightly browned. Add onion, carrot, chopped celery and garlic to bacon. Cook, stirring occasionally, until beginning to brown. Add ground beef; cook, stirring occasionally, until evenly browned. Stir in chicken livers; cook until they are no longer pink. Drain off excess fat. Stir in tomato paste, wine, stock and seasonings. Cover and bring to a boil. Cook over low heat 30 to 40 minutes. Serve with spaghetti. Garnish with celery leaves, if desired. Makes about 3 cups.

Cannelloni au Gratin

1/4 cup butter
1 medium-size onion, finely chopped
1 garlic clove, crushed
6 cups sliced mushrooms (12 oz.)
1 tablespoon all-purpose flour
3/4 cup crème fraîche
Salt, pepper and nutmeg
Herb Pasta using 1 egg, see pages 10-11
6 very thin prosciutto slices
1/2 cup fresh bread crumbs
1/4 cup grated Parmesan cheese (3/4 oz.)
Additional proscuitto slice, if desired
Fresh mint, if desired

In a medium-size saucepan over low heat, melt butter. Add onion and garlic; cook until soft. Add mushrooms; cook, stirring, until soft and most of liquid has evaporated. Stir in flour; add 1/3 cup of crème fraîche to form a thick sauce. Season with salt, pepper and nutmeg. Preheat oven to 350F (175C). Roll out pasta, see page 12; cut out 6 (5" x 4") rectangles. Put a prosciutto slice on each rectangle, spoon some mushroom filling across each 1 and roll up from short end. Pack tightly, seams down, in a greased 1-1/2-quart oblong baking dish. Pour remaining crème fraîche over top and sprinkle with mixed bread crumbs and Parmesan cheese. Bake 20 minutes or until golden and bubbling. Garnish with additional proscuitto slice and mint, if desired. Makes 6 first-course servings.

— Spinach & Ham Cannelloni —

1 lb. fresh spinach
2 tablespoons butter
1 medium-size onion, finely chopped
1 tablespoon all-purpose flour
2/3 cup milk
4 oz. ham, finely chopped (1/2 cup)
Salt, pepper and nutmeg
8 ready-to-use cannelloni tubes
1 recipe Béchamel Sauce, see
    page 48
3/4 cup grated Cheddar cheese (3 oz.)
2 (1-oz.) ham slices, cut in strips, if
    desired
Fresh bay leaves, if desired

In a medium-size covered saucepan, cook spinach in a little water until tender. Drain thoroughly. Chop until fine. In the same saucepan over medium heat, melt butter. Add onion and cook until soft. Stir in flour and cook 1 minute. Gradually stir in milk; boil 1 minute. Stir in spinach, chopped ham, salt, pepper and nutmeg. Using a teaspoon, push spinach mixture into cannelloni tubes. Preheat oven to 425F (220C). In a small saucepan, heat Béchamel Sauce over low heat. Stir in 1/2 cup of the cheese. Pour 1/2 of the sauce into a greased oblong 1-quart baking dish. Arrange cannelloni in a single layer in dish; pour remaining sauce over top. Bake 40 minutes or until golden and bubbling. Arrange ham strips in a lattice pattern on top, if desired, and sprinkle with remaining cheese. Garnish with bay leaves, if desired. Makes 4 servings.

Lobster Shells

Meat from a 1 lb. lobster
2 teaspoons lemon juice
2/3 cup whipping cream
Salt
Red (cayenne) pepper
8 conchiglie (large shells), cooked
1/2 teaspoon grated lemon peel
2 teaspoons chopped fresh dill
Black pepper
Lemon twists, if desired
Fresh dill, if desired

Preheat oven to 375F (190C). Chop lobster meat in coarse pieces. Put into a bowl with lemon juice and 2 tablespoons of whipping cream. Season with salt and red pepper. Mix well together. Fill shells with lobster mixture. Arrange in a greased 1-1/2-quart oblong baking dish. In a bowl, mix together remaining whipping cream, lemon peel and dill. Season with salt and black pepper. Pour over shells. Cover dish with foil. Bake 15 to 20 minutes or until heated through. Baste with sauce halfway through cooking time. Garnish with lemon twists and dill, if desired. Makes 4 first-course servings.

—— Fish Ravioli in Leek Sauce ——

8 oz. white fish fillets, such as cod,
  cooked, flaked
2 canned anchovies, drained, minced
1/4 cup grated Parmesan
  cheese (3/4 oz.)
Grated peel and juice of 1/2 lemon
1 egg yolk
Pepper and nutmeg
Fresh Pasta, using 3 eggs,
  see page 10
Chopped fresh parsley, if desired
Blanched shredded leek, if desired
Lemon peel strips, if desired

Leek Sauce:
1 lb. leeks, sliced
1/4 cup butter
2/3 cup fish or Chicken Stock, see
  page 27
2/3 cup dairy sour cream

In a medium-size bowl, mix fish, anchovies, Parmesan cheese, lemon peel and juice and egg yolk. Season with pepper and nutmeg. Process in a blender or food processor until fairly smooth. Roll out pasta dough and, using fish purée as a filling, make ravioli; see page 16. Make sauce. Drop ravioli into boiling water and cook 8 to 10 minutes. Drain and turn into a heated serving dish. Warm sauce and pour over ravioli. Garnish with parsley, leek and lemon peel strips, if desired. Makes 6 first-course servings.

To make sauce: Melt butter in a medium-size saucepan. Add leeks and stir until coated with butter. Cover pan and cook gently until leeks are soft; add stock. Process mixture in a blender or food processor until smooth. Stir in sour cream.

— Pasta with Spinach & Ricotta —

1 lb. spinach
2 cups ricotta cheese (8 oz.)
1/2 cup grated Parmesan
   cheese (1-1/2 oz.)
1 egg yolk
Salt, pepper and nutmeg
Fresh Pasta, using 3 eggs,
   see page 10
1/3 cup butter
2 tablespoons chopped fresh mixed
   herbs (about 1/2 teaspoon dried
   mixed herbs)
2 teaspoons lemon juice

In a large saucepan, cook spinach in a
small amount of water until tender.
Drain; cool. Squeeze spinach dry;
chop in a blender or food processor.
Add ricotta cheese, Parmesan cheese,
egg yolk, salt, pepper and nutmeg.
Process until fairly smooth. Roll out
pasta; see page 12. Cut in 2-inch

squares. Put 1/2 teaspoon of filling in
middle of each square. Fold in half to
make a triangle; press edges to seal.
Wrap long side of triangle around
index finger; press ends together.
Leave on a towel to dry, turning after
1 hour. Cook cappelletti in a large
saucepan of boiling water 10 to 15
minutes or until tender but firm. In a
small saucepan, melt butter; stir in
herbs and lemon juice. Drain cappelletti; put into a heated serving dish.
Add herb butter sauce; stir thoroughly. Serve at once. Makes 6 first-course
servings, 4 main-course servings.

Variation
Use Pasta Verde or Tomato Pasta, see
page 11, to make a mixture of different colored pasta. If desired, cut pasta in 2-inch circles instead of squares.

Ravioli with Butter & Sage

1/3 cup butter
1 medium-size onion, chopped
8 oz. ground pork
8 oz. ground veal
2 tablespoons tomato paste, dissolved
   in 1/4 cup water
Salt, pepper and nutmeg
1/2 cup fresh bread crumbs
2 egg yolks
1 cup grated Parmesan cheese (3 oz.)
Fresh Pasta, using 3 eggs,
   see page 10
Fresh sage leaves

To make filling, in a medium-size saucepan, melt 2 tablespoons of butter; add onion and cook until soft. Add meat; cook, stirring until brown. Stir in tomato paste mixture and season with salt, pepper and nutmeg. Cover and simmer 30 minutes. Cool, then process in a blender or food processor until smooth, adding bread crumbs, egg yolks and cheese. Make ravioli; see page 16, filling with meat mixture. Drop ravioli into boiling salted water and cook 15 to 20 minutes or until tender but firm. Drain and place in a heated serving dish. Melt remaining butter, pour over ravioli. Season with pepper and garnish with sage leaves. Serve at once. Makes 6 first-course servings.

Tortellini in Tomato Sauce

2 cups cooked chopped chicken
1/2 cup mortadella (4 oz.)
2 eggs
1/2 cup grated Parmesan
  cheese (1-1/2 oz.)
Salt, pepper and nutmeg
Fresh Pasta, using 3 eggs,
  see page 10
1 recipe Tomato Sauce, see page 45
Additional grated Parmesan cheese, if
  desired

In a blender or food processor, chop chicken and mortadella until fine. Add eggs, 1/2 cup Parmesan cheese, salt, pepper and nutmeg; process until fairly smooth. Roll out pasta; see page 12. Using a biscuit cutter, cut out rounds 1-1/2 inches in diameter. Put 1/2 teaspoon of filling in middle of each round. Fold each round in half over filling so that upper edge comes just short of lower edge. Press edges to seal. Curl around index finger, pressing two parts firmly together. Leave on a towel to dry, turning after 1 hour. Cook tortellini in a large saucepan of boiling salted water about 10 minutes or until tender but firm. In a small saucepan, heat Tomato Sauce. Drain tortellini, place in a heated serving dish and pour sauce over top. Sprinkle with additional Parmesan cheese, if desired, and serve. Makes 6 first-course servings, 4 main-course servings.

Vermicelli Flan

2 tablespoons butter
2 small leeks, sliced
6 bacon slices, chopped
4 oz. vermicelli
1/2 cup grated Cheddar cheese (2 oz.)
2/3 cup plain yogurt
2/3 cup half and half
2 eggs, beaten
Salt and pepper
1 medium-size tomato, sliced
Leek leaves, if desired

In a skillet, melt butter. Add leeks and bacon. Cook gently until leeks are tender. Preheat oven to 375F (190C). In a large pan of boiling salted water, cook vermicelli until just tender to the bite. Drain; return to pan. Stir in cheese. Press vermicelli onto bottom and sides of a well-greased 9-inch flan pan. Spread bacon and sliced leeks over pasta base. In a medium-size bowl, beat together yogurt, half and half, eggs, salt and pepper. Pour over bacon and leeks. Arrange tomato slices on top. Bake 30 minutes, or until puffed and golden brown. Remove flan ring and serve warm or cold. Garnish with leek leaves, if desired. Makes 4 servings.

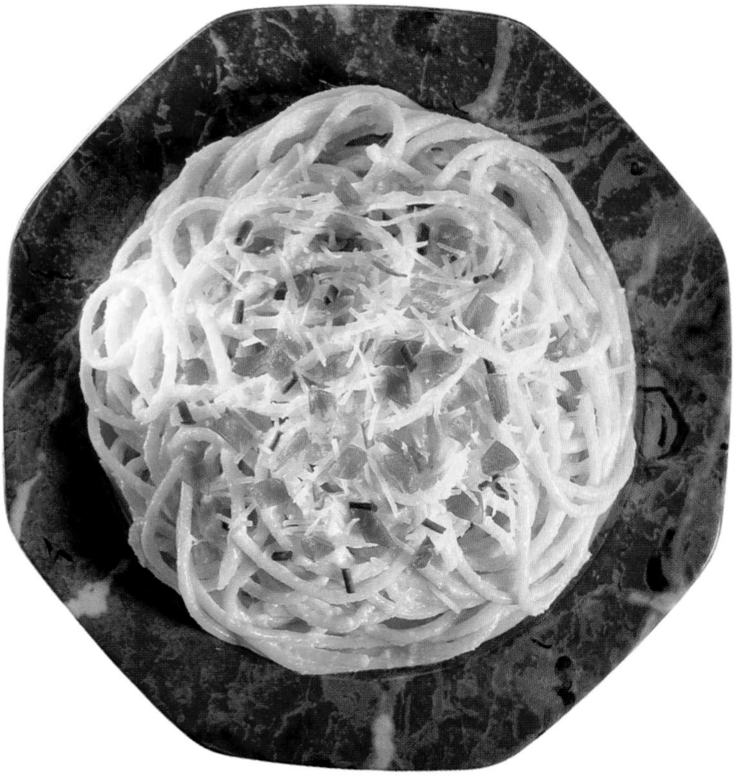

— Bucatini with Four Cheeses —

6 oz. bucatini
1-1/4 cups half and half
1/2 cup grated Parmesan
  cheese (1-1/2 oz.)
3 oz. Gruyère cheese, cut into small
  dice
3 oz. soft goat's cheese
3 oz. mozzarella cheese, cut into
  small dice
Pepper
Chopped ham, if desired
Chopped chives, if desired

In a large saucepan of boiling salted water, cook bucatini until just tender to the bite. Drain bucatini. Put half and half in a large saucepan with half of Parmesan cheese. Add Gruyère cheese, goat's cheese and mozzarella cheese. Cook over low heat until cheeses are melted. Season with pepper. Add drained bucatini to cheese mixture. Stir well. Sprinkle with remaining Parmesan cheese, ham and chives, if desired. Serve at once. Makes 4 servings.

Lasagne

8 oz. lasagne noodles
1 recipe Béchamel Sauce, see page 48
4 oz. mozzarella cheese, cubed
1 recipe Bolognese Sauce, see page 51
2 tablespoons grated Parmesan cheese
Zucchini slices, if desired
Shredded radicchio, if desired
Endive leaves, if desired

In a large saucepan of boiling salted water, cook noodles, in 2 batches, about 10 minutes or until just tender to the bite. Drain thoroughly. Spread out on paper towels. Preheat oven to 350F (175C). In a saucepan, heat Béchamel Sauce. Add mozzarella cheese; stir until melted. Arrange a noodle layer in bottom of a greased 3-quart oblong baking dish. Spoon half of Bolognese Sauce over top. Cover with noodles. Spread with half of cheese sauce. Repeat layers finishing with remaining cheese sauce. Sprinkle with Parmesan cheese. Bake 30 to 40 minutes or until bubbly. Garnish with zucchini slices, radicchio and endive leaves, if desired, and serve. Makes 4 to 6 servings.

Spinach Pasta Roll

1 tablespoon vegetable oil
1 medium-size onion, finely chopped
2 (10 oz.) pkgs. frozen chopped
   spinach, thawed, drained
2/3 cup cottage cheese
1 cup grated Parmesan cheese (3 oz.)
1 egg yolk
Salt and pepper
1 recipe Fresh Pasta, see page 10
1/4 cup butter
Watercress, if desired

In a 10-inch skillet, heat oil. Add onion; cook until soft. Add spinach; cook 2 minutes, stirring frequently. In a large bowl, mix together cottage cheese, 1/2 of Parmesan cheese, egg yolk, salt and pepper. Stir in spinach and onion. Roll pasta dough in a 14" x 12" rectangle, joining 2 sheets of pasta together if necessary and moistening seam with water. Spread with spinach mixture, leaving a 1/2-inch border around edge. Roll up from long edge. Cut in half to make 2 rolls. Wrap each roll in waxed paper, then foil, leaving seam at top. Turn up ends of foil to form handles. Lay rolls in a deep 10-inch skillet with a cover; add enough water to come halfway up rolls. Bring to a boil; reduce heat. Cover and simmer rolls 30 minutes. Remove from pan; unwrap and cool. Preheat oven to 375F (190C). Cut rolls in 3/4-inch slices. Arrange in a shallow baking dish large enough to hold slices in 1 layer. Melt butter; pour over slices. Sprinkle with remaining Parmesan cheese. Bake 15 minutes or until golden. Garnish with watercress, if desired. Makes 4 servings.

Fish & Pasta Ring

6 oz. tagliatelle verde
2 tablespoons butter
4 eggs, beaten
1-1/4 cups milk
Salt, pepper and nutmeg
1 recipe Tomato Sauce, see page 45
1 lb. white fish fillets, such as cod,
    skinned, cubed
Fresh bay leaves, if desired

In a large saucepan of boiling salted water, cook tagliatelle until just tender to the bite. Drain. Preheat oven to 350F (175C). In a small saucepan, melt butter. Brush a 1-1/2-quart ring mold generously with 1/2 of the melted butter. In a medium-size bowl, beat together eggs, milk, salt, pepper, nutmeg and remaining butter. Pour mixture into buttered ring mold. Spoon drained tagliatelle into ring mold and arrange evenly. Bake in oven 40 minutes or until set. Pour Tomato Sauce into a medium-size saucepan. Bring to a boil; add fish. Simmer gently, uncovered, 5 to 10 minutes or until fish is opaque. Turn out pasta ring onto a large heated serving dish. Spoon some fish sauce into the center; pour a little over top of pasta ring. Arrange remaining fish and sauce around the edge. Garnish with bay leaves, if desired. Makes 4 servings.

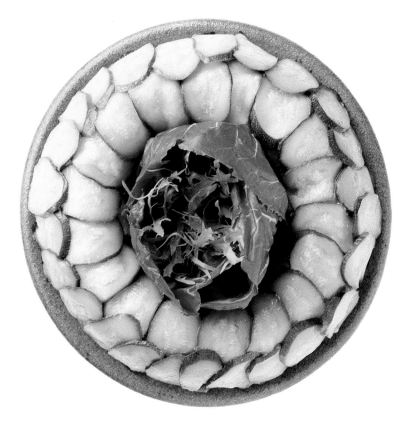

Zucchini & Pasta Mold

3 medium-size zucchini, thinly sliced
2-1/4 cups whole-wheat ears (4 oz.)
2 tablespoons vegetable oil
1 large onion, finely chopped
4 medium-size tomatoes, peeled,
  chopped
1 tablespoon tomato paste
2 teaspoons chopped fresh oregano
1 egg, beaten
Salt and pepper
2 tablespoons butter
Radicchio, if desired
Endive leaves, if desired

In a pan of boiling water, cook zucchini 3 to 4 minutes or until crisp-tender. Drain; rinse with cold water. Pat dry with paper towels. In a large pan of boiling salted water, cook pasta until just tender to the bite. Drain. Meanwhile, heat oil in a 6-inch skillet. Add onions; cook gently until soft. In a large bowl, mix together pasta, cooked onion, tomatoes, tomato paste, oregano, egg, salt and pepper. Preheat oven to 400F (205C). Line a well-buttered 2-quart ring mold with zucchini slices, overlapping them like tiles on a roof. Fill mold with pasta mixture. Cover with overlapping zucchini slices. Dot with butter. Cover with foil. Bake 40 minutes or until pasta mixture is set. Turn out onto a serving plate. Serve hot or cold. Garnish with radicchio and endive leaves, if desired. Makes 6 servings.

—— Smoked Fish Lasagne ——

**1 lb. smoked fish fillets, such
  as haddock
2 cups milk
4 medium-size carrots, cut in
  small dice
4 celery stalks, cut in small dice
1/3 cup butter
2 cups water
6 lasagne verde noodles
1 tablespoon chopped fresh parsley
Salt and pepper
1/2 cup all-purpose flour
Nutmeg
2 tablespoons Parmesan cheese, grated
Lemon slices, if desired
Fresh parsley, if desired**

Put fish and milk into a medium-size saucepan. Bring to a boil; reduce heat to low and cook until fish flakes. Combine carrots and celery in a medium-size saucepan with 3 tablespoons of butter and water. Bring to a boil; simmer until vegetables are tender. Meanwhile, in a large saucepan of boiling salted water, cook noodles until just tender to the bite. Drain; spread out on paper towels. Drain fish, reserving cooking liquid. Flake fish into a bowl. Drain vegetables, reserving cooking liquid. Add vegetables to fish with chopped parsley. Season with salt and pepper. Preheat oven to 375F (190C). Make a Béchamel Sauce, see page 48, with reserved fish and vegetable cooking liquids, remaining butter and flour. Season with salt, pepper and nutmeg. Put a layer of noodles in bottom of a greased 2-quart oblong baking dish. Cover with a third of fish mixture, then a third of sauce. Repeat layers twice, ending with sauce. Sprinkle with Parmesan cheese. Bake 25 minutes or until hot and bubbly. Garnish with lemon slices and parsley, if desired, and serve. Makes 4 to 6 servings.

Smoked Fish Mousse

1 tablespoon butter
24 peeled deveined shrimp
Fennel leaves
12 oz. smoked fish fillets, such
   as haddock, skinned, cut
   into pieces
3 egg whites
1/2 pint whipping cream (1 cup)
Salt and red (cayenne) pepper
1 cup small pasta shells (2 oz.), cooked
Lumpfish roe, if desired
Lime slices, if desired

Preheat oven to 350F (175C). Butter 6 (10-ounce) ramekins. Place 4 shrimp and a piece of fennel in bottom of each dish. In a blender or food processor, process fish until smooth. Mix in egg whites and cream. Season with salt and a pinch of red pepper. Stir in pasta shells. Divide mixture among ramekins. Place dishes in a baking pan. Pour in water to come halfway up dishes. Bake about 15 minutes or until firm. Turn out onto serving plates. Garnish with roe and lime slices, if desired. Makes 6 first-course servings.

—— Tuna & Macaroni Layer ——

1-1/4 cups whole-wheat macaroni
(6 oz.), cooked
3/4 cup shredded Cheddar cheese
(3 oz.)
1 (7-oz.) can tuna, drained
1/2 recipe Béchamel Sauce,
see page 48
2 teaspoons lemon juice
2 hard-cooked eggs, chopped
1 tablespoon chopped fresh parsley
Salt and pepper
Lemon pieces, if desired
Fresh parsley, if desired

Mix macaroni with 1/2 cup of cheese. Set aside. Flake tuna into a small saucepan with Béchamel Sauce, lemon juice, eggs, chopped parsley, salt and pepper. Toss together. Cook over low heat until warmed through. Divide tuna mixture among 4 (10-ounce) flameproof ramekins. Top with macaroni and cheese mixture. Sprinkle remaining 1/4 cup of cheese over top. Broil under medium heat until golden and bubbling. Garnish with lemon pieces and parsley, if desired. Makes 4 servings.

Kidney & Pasta Turbigo

4 lamb kidneys.
1/4 cup butter
4 cocktail sausages
4 oz. button mushrooms (2 cups)
24 button onions, peeled
1 teaspoon tomato paste
2 teaspoons all-purpose flour
2/3 cup beef stock
1 tablespoon dry sherry
1 bay leaf
Salt and pepper
3 cups pasta spirals (6 oz.)

Skin and cut kidneys in half; remove core. In a medium-size saucepan, melt butter. Add kidneys and sausages. Cook over medium heat, stirring occasionally, until brown. Remove from pan; set aside. Add mushrooms and onions to saucepan. Cook 5 to 6 minutes, stirring occasionally. Stir in tomato paste and flour. Cook 1 to 2 minutes. Stir in stock and sherry. Bring to a boil. Return kidneys and sausages to saucepan with bay leaf. Add salt and pepper. Cover pan. Reduce heat to low; cook 20 to 25 minutes or until kidneys are tender. Meanwhile, in a large saucepan of boiling salted water, cook pasta until just tender to the bite. Drain. Add to kidney mixture, toss to coat pasta. Makes 4 servings.

– Tomato & Zucchini Pasta Bake –

3 medium-size zucchini, sliced
4 cups rigatoni (12 oz.)
1 recipe Tomato Sauce, see page 45
8 oz. mozzarella cheese, thinly sliced
1 teaspoon olive oil
Fresh basil, if desired

Bring a small amount of water to a boil in a medium-size saucepan. Add sliced zucchini and cook for a few minutes until crisp-tender. Drain; set aside. Preheat oven to 350F (175C). In a large saucepan of boiling salted water, cook rigatoni until almost tender. Drain; rinse in cold water. Place 1/3 of rigatoni in a buttered 3-quart oblong baking dish. Spread 1/3 of Tomato Sauce, followed by 1/3 of cheese over rigatoni. Repeat layers, then spread zucchini over cheese. Cover with remaining rigatoni, Tomato Sauce and cheese. Sprinkle with olive oil. Bake 20 minutes or until cheese has melted over top. Garnish with basil, if desired. Makes 4 to 6 servings.

Pork & Beans

2 tablespoons vegetable oil
3/4 lb. pork tenderloin, cut in thin
  slices
1 medium-size onion, chopped
1 garlic clove, crushed
1-1/4 cups whole-wheat pasta grills
  (6 oz.)
1 (15-oz.) can cannellini beans (white
  kidney beans), drained
3 tablespoons chopped fresh parsley
3 tablepoons tomato paste
1 quart Chicken Stock, see page 27
Salt and pepper
Additional chopped fresh parsley, if
  desired

In a deep 10-inch skillet with a cover, heat oil. Add pork; cook over medium heat until browned. Remove pork from pan. Set aside. Add onion and garlic to pan; cook until beginning to soften. Return pork to pan, stir in pasta, beans, 3 tablespoons chopped parsley, tomato paste, stock, salt and pepper. Bring to a boil; reduce heat. Cover pan. Simmer, stirring occasionally, about 20 minutes or until pasta is tender and most of liquid is absorbed. Add more stock if liquid is absorbed before pasta is cooked. Sprinkle with additional chopped parsley, if desired, and serve. Makes 6 first-course servings, 4 main-course servings.

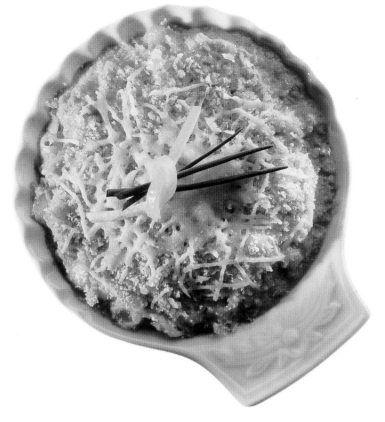

Devilled Crab

8 oz. crabmeat
1 teaspoon Dijon-style mustard
2 teaspoons Worcestershire sauce
Juice of 1/2 lemon
Salt and red (cayenne) pepper
1/2 cup plain yogurt
1 cup small pasta shells (2 oz.), cooked
2 tablespoons fresh bread crumbs
1/4 cup grated Parmesan
  cheese (3/4 oz.)
Lemon peel strip, if desired
Chives, if desired

Preheat broiler. In a medium-size
bowl, combine crabmeat, mustard,
Worcestershire sauce, lemon juice,
yogurt and pasta. Season with salt
and red pepper. Divide mixture
among 6 scallop shells. In a small
bowl, mix together bread crumbs and
Parmesan cheese. Sprinkle crumbs
over crab mixture. Broil under
medium heat about 10 minutes or
until golden. Garnish with lemon
peel strip and chives, if desired.
Makes 6 first-course servings.

Frankfurter Bake

2 tablespoons vegetable oil
1 onion, sliced
2 celery stalks, sliced
6 frankfurters, cut in 1-inch lengths
2 tomatoes, peeled, chopped
2 teaspoons cornstarch
2/3 cup dairy sour cream
1 tablespoon tomato paste
Salt and pepper
3 cups pasta wheels (6 oz.), cooked
Additional sour cream, if desired
Fresh parsley, if desired

In a deep 10-inch skillet, heat oil. Add onion, celery and frankfurters. Cook, stirring occasionally, until onions and celery are soft. Add tomatoes. Cook 5 more minutes. Preheat oven to 425F (220C). In a small bowl, blend cornstarch and a little of the 2/3 cup of sour cream. Stir in remaining 2/3 cup of sour cream. Add to vegetables in skillet with tomato paste, salt and pepper. Stir pasta into vegetable mixture. Pour into a buttered 2-quart oblong dish. Bake 10 minutes or until bubbly. Garnish with additional sour cream and parsley, if desired. Makes 4 servings.

Vermicelli Timbal

4 oz. fine vermicelli
1/2 recipe Béchamel Sauce,
  see page 48
4 oz. mozzarella cheese
4 oz. ham
1 tablespoon butter
1/4 cup fresh bread crumbs
1 recipe Tomato Sauce, see page 45
Fresh mint, if desired

In a large saucepan of boiling salted water, cook vermicelli until just tender to the bite. Drain. In a medium-size bowl, combine drained vermicelli and Béchamel Sauce. Set aside. Preheat oven to 425F (220C). Butter 6 (6-ounce) custard cups. Coat with 1/2 of bread crumbs. Cut cheese and ham in small dice. Half fill each custard cup with pasta mixture. Divide cheese and ham among cups. Fill cups with pasta mixture. Sprinkle tops with remaining bread crumbs. Bake 15 minutes or until bubbly. Run a sharp knife around inside of cups. Turn out onto warmed serving plates. Serve with Tomato Sauce. Garnish with mint, if desired. Makes 6 servings.

Baked Cod Italienne

2 tablespoons butter
2 cups sliced mushrooms (4 oz.)
1 recipe Tomato Sauce, see page 45
4 (4- to 5-oz.) white fish steaks,
    such as cod
Salt and pepper
1 cup pasta shells (4 oz.)
8 ripe olives

Preheat oven to 375F (190C). In a medium-size saucepan, melt butter. Add mushrooms; cook gently until soft. Stir in Tomato Sauce. Put fish into a buttered 2-quart oblong baking dish. Season with salt and pepper. Pour tomato and mushroom sauce over fish. Cover dish with foil; bake about 25 minutes or until fish is opaque when tested with a fork. Meanwhile, cook pasta, see page 7, until just tender to the bite. About 5 minutes before fish has finished cooking, arrange pasta around fish, spooning some of sauce over pasta. Garnish with olives and serve. Makes 4 servings.

Broccoli Pasta Soufflé

8 oz. broccoli
3 tablespoons butter
3 tablespoons all-purpose flour
1-1/4 cups milk
3/4 cup shredded Cheddar
cheese (3 oz.)
Salt, pepper and nutmeg
4 egg whites
3 egg yolks
2 cups pasta shells (4 oz.), cooked

Divide broccoli in small flowerets. Cook in a medium-size saucepan in a small amount of boiling salted water until crisp-tender. Drain. Preheat oven to 400F (205C). In a large saucepan, melt butter; stir in flour. Cook 2 minutes, stirring constantly, over low heat. Gradually stir in milk. Cook, stirring constantly, until sauce thickens. Simmer gently 5 minutes. Stir in cheese. Season with salt, pepper and nutmeg. Let cool slightly. In a large bowl, whisk egg whites until stiff but not dry. Stir egg yolks into cheese sauce, then stir in broccoli and pasta. Stir 1 tablespoon of egg whites into mixture; gently fold in remaining egg whites. Grease a 2-quart soufflé dish (7-3/4" x 3-3/4"). Pour in mixture; bake about 30 minutes or until soufflé is well risen, golden brown and just set in middle. Serve at once. Makes 4 servings.

Note: This mixture may be baked in individual soufflé dishes 20 minutes.

──── Bolognese Soufflé ────

**3 cups whole-wheat pasta spirals
(about 4-1/2 oz.)
1 recipe Bolognese Sauce, see page 51
3 eggs, separated
1/4 cup grated Parmesan
cheese (3/4 oz.)**

Preheat oven to 375F (190C). In a
large saucepan of boiling salted
water, cook pasta until just tender to
the bite. Drain well. Stir into Bolognese Sauce. Stir egg yolks into pasta
mixture. In a medium-size bowl, beat
egg whites until stiff. Gently fold into
pasta mixture. Grease a 3-quart soufflé dish. Pour soufflé mixture into
greased dish. Sprinkle with Parmesan cheese. Bake 40 minutes or until
well risen and golden brown. Serve at
once. Makes 4 servings.

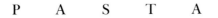

Pepper Gratin

2 large red bell peppers
2 large yellow bell peppers
1/2 cup olive oil
1 garlic clove, crushed
4 anchovey fillets, drained, chopped
8 pitted ripe olives, chopped
1 tablespoon capers
Salt and pepper
8 oz. spaghetti
2 tablespoons fresh bread crumbs
2 tablespoons grated Parmesan cheese
Green bell pepper strips, if desired
Additional ripe olives, if desired

Cook bell peppers under broiler. Turn peppers at intervals until skins are blistered and blackened. Cool in a paper bag. Preheat oven to 375F (190C). Scrape off skins of bell peppers; cut in strips. In a 10-inch skillet, heat 1/4 cup of olive oil. Add cooked bell pepper strips and garlic. Cook 2 to 3 minutes or until softened. Stir in anchovies, chopped olives and capers. Season with salt and pepper. In a large saucepan of boiling salted water, cook spaghetti, see pages 7-8. Drain and return to pan. Toss with 2 tablespoons of remaining olive oil. Combine bread crumbs and Parmesan cheese; sprinkle half of mixture over bottom of a 2-quart oblong baking dish. Spoon half of bell-pepper mixture over bread-crumb mixture. Cover with cooked spaghetti. Spoon remaining bell-pepper mixture over spaghetti, then sprinkle with remaining bread-crumb mixture. Drizzle with remaining 2 tablespoons of olive oil. Bake 20 minutes or until golden brown. Garnish with bell pepper strips and additional olives, if desired. Makes 4 servings.

Turkey Tetrazzini

1/4 cup butter
4 (1-oz.) thin ham slices, chopped
1 onion, finely chopped
2 cups sliced mushrooms (4 oz.)
1/3 cup all-purpose flour
1-3/4 cups Chicken Stock, see page 27
2/3 cup whipping cream
2 tablespoons dry sherry
2 cups cubed cooked turkey
8 oz. red, green and white tagliatelle, cooked
Salt, pepper and nutmeg
1/4 cup grated Parmesan cheese (3/4 oz.)
Fresh parsley, if desired

Preheat oven to 350F (175C). In a medium-size saucepan, melt butter over medium heat. Add ham and onion. Cook until onion is soft. Add mushrooms; cook until soft. Stir in flour; cook, stirring constantly, 2 minutes. Gradually stir in stock. Simmer, stirring constantly, until sauce is thickened and smooth. Remove pan from heat. Stir in whipping cream, sherry, turkey and tagliatelle. Season with salt, pepper and nutmeg. Pour into a greased 2-quart baking dish. Sprinkle with Parmesan cheese. Bake 30 minutes or until golden brown. Garnish with parsley, if desired. Makes 4 servings.

Sweet & Sour Pork

2 lbs. lean boneless pork
2 tablespoons vegetable oil
1 onion, sliced
1 teaspoon ground ginger
1 tablespoon all-purpose flour
1 (8-oz.) can pineapple tidbits in juice
1-1/2 cups Chicken Stock, see page 27
1-1/4 cups dry cider
2 tablespoons soy sauce
2 teaspoons Worcestershire sauce
2 tablespoons brown sugar
2 tablespoons white wine vinegar
Salt and pepper
2 cups small pasta shells (2 oz.)
Green bell pepper slices, if desired
Green onion daisies, if desired

Cut pork in 1-inch cubes. Preheat oven to 300F (150C). Heat oil in a 3-quart flameproof casserole dish. Add pork and cook until well browned, stirring occasionally. Remove from dish; set aside. Add onion to dish; cook until soft. Stir in ginger and flour and cook 2 minutes. Drain juice from pineapple. Set pineapple aside. Add juice to onion mixture with stock, cider, soy sauce, Worcestershire sauce, brown sugar and vinegar. Season with salt and pepper; stir well. Return meat to dish. Cover and bake 30 minutes. Stir in reserved pineapple and pasta. Cover and bake 30 minutes or until pasta is just tender to the bite. Garnish with bell pepper slices and green onion daisies, if desired. Makes 4 to 6 servings.

Fish & Pasta Pie

12 oz. smoked haddock
12 oz. fresh haddock
1-3/4 cups milk
1-1/4 cups water
2 tablespoons butter
2 tablespoons all-purpose flour
1 teaspoon lemon juice
3 hard-cooked eggs, sliced
Salt and pepper
1 tablespoon chopped fresh parsley
1 cup plain yogurt (8 oz.)
2 eggs, beaten
1-3/4 cups macaroni (6 oz.), cooked
1 cup shredded Cheddar
   Cheese (4 oz.)
Lemon slices, if desired, cut in half
Fresh parsley, if desired

Put smoked and fresh haddock in a medium-size saucepan with milk and water. Poach 5 to 10 minutes until fresh haddock is opaque when tested with a fork. Reserve 1-1/4 cups of cooking liquid. Preheat oven to 375F (190C). Melt butter in a medium-size saucepan. Stir in flour; cook, stirring constantly, 2 minutes. Stir in reserved cooking liquid. Cook until thickened, stirring constantly. Add fish, lemon juice, hard-cooked eggs and chopped parsley. Season with salt and pepper. Pour mixture into a 2-quart casserole. In a medium-size bowl, mix together yogurt and beaten eggs. Stir in macaroni and 1/3 cup of cheese. Pour over fish mixture. Sprinkle with remaining cheese. Bake 25 to 30 minutes or until golden brown. Garnish with lemon slices and parsley, if desired. Makes 4 to 6 servings.

Oriental Lamb Casserole

1 tablespoon vegetable oil
1-1/2 lbs. boneless lamb, cut in 1-inch
  cubes
1 onion, cut in wedges
1 carrot, cut into julienne strips
1 green bell pepper, cut into strips
1 red bell pepper, cut into strips
12 oz. white cabbage, shredded
  (3 cups)
2 tablespoons soy sauce
1 tablespoon Worcestershire sauce
2 tablespoons white wine vinegar
1 tablespoon honey
2 cups light beef stock
1 tablespoon chopped fresh parsley
Salt and pepper
2 oz. round egg noodles
Crispy noodles, if desired
Additional chopped fresh parsley, if
  desired

Heat oil in a large saucepan and add lamb. Cook over medium heat until brown, stirring occasionally. Add onion, carrot, bell peppers and shredded cabbage to lamb. Stir well; cover and cook over low heat 5 minutes. In a medium-size bowl, mix together soy sauce, Worcestershire sauce, vinegar, honey, stock and 1 tablespoon chopped parsley. Stir into lamb mixture. Season with salt and pepper. Cook, covered, stirring occasionally, about 50 minutes. Add egg noodles and cook 10 minutes or until noodles are tender. Garnish with crispy noodles and additional chopped parsley, if desired, and serve. Makes 4 servings.

Stuffed Peppers

1 cup pasta spirals (2 oz.), cooked
1/2 recipe Tomato Sauce, see page 45
2 teaspoons capers
6 pitted ripe olives, chopped
2 red bell peppers
2 yellow bell peppers
2 teaspoons olive oil
Fresh basil leaves, if desired

Preheat oven to 375F (190C). In a medium-size bowl, mix together pasta, Tomato Sauce, capers and olives. Slice off the stem end of peppers. Remove core and seeds. Fill peppers with pasta and tomato mixture. Replace tops of peppers. Put peppers in a buttered 1-1/2-quart oblong baking dish. Pour a little olive oil over each. Bake about 30 minutes or until peppers are tender. Garnish with basil leaves, if desired, and serve. Makes 4 servings.

Beef & Macaroni Strudel

1 cup macaroni (4 oz.)
2 tablespoons vegetable oil
1 onion, finely chopped
8 oz. lean ground beef
1 tablespoon tomato paste
1/2 teaspoon ground cinnamon
1 tablespoon chopped fresh parsley
Salt and pepper
1/2 recipe Béchamel Sauce, see page
  48
1/4 cup butter
4 sheets filo pastry
Tomato wedges, if desired
Onion slices, if desired, separated in
  rings
Fresh parsley, if desired

In a large saucepan of boiling salted water, cook macaroni until just tender to the bite. Drain macaroni. Preheat oven to 375F (190C). In a 10-inch skillet, heat oil. Add onion; cook until soft. Add beef; stir until evenly browned. Drain off excess fat. Stir in tomato paste, cinnamon, chopped parsley, salt and pepper. Stir cooked macaroni into beef mixture with Béchamel Sauce. In a small saucepan, melt butter. Brush a sheet of filo pastry with butter. Lay another sheet of pastry on top. Brush with more butter. Repeat with remaining pastry. Place macaroni mixture in a line along 1 long edge of pastry, leaving a space at each end. Tuck ends over, roll up firmly. Place on a large baking sheet. Brush rolls with butter. Bake 45 minutes or until brown and crisp, brushing with butter occasionally. Garnish with tomato wedges, onion rings and parsley, if desired, and serve. Makes 4 servings.

Variation
Make individual strudels, if desired, and bake for 20 to 25 minutes.

Mongolian Hot Pot

2 oz. transparent noodles
1 lb. boneless skinned chicken breasts
1 lb. beef round steak
1 (8-oz.) can bamboo shoots, drained
4 oz. Chinese cabbage, shredded
    (2-1/2 cups)
2 cups button mushrooms (4 oz.)
Sauce, see below
1 quart Chicken Stock, see page 27
1 (1-inch) cube ginger root, grated
1 garlic clove, crushed
4 green onions, chopped

Sauce:
3 tablespoons hot water
2 tablespoons peanut butter
2 tablespoons soy sauce
2 tablespoons dry sherry
Pinch of chili powder
Hot-pepper slices, if desired

In a medium-size bowl of warm water, soak noodles 5 minutes. Drain; set aside. Cut chicken, steak and bamboo shoots in very thin strips. Arrange on a flat dish with cabbage and mushrooms. Make sauce. To serve, in a medium-size saucepan or fondue pot, bring chicken stock to a boil. Add ginger, garlic and onions. Place pot over heat at table. Dip meat and vegetables into stock to cook; eat with sauce. Add noodles to stock; allow to heat through. Serve stock and noodles in soup bowls. Makes 4 servings.

To make sauce: In a small bowl, mix water with peanut butter. Stir in soy sauce, sherry and chili powder. Garnish with hot-pepper, if desired.

— Spicy Vegetables & Noodles —

2 tablespoons vegetable oil
1 garlic clove, crushed
1 (1/2-inch) cube ginger root, grated
1/2 lb. spinach, coarsely chopped
8 oz. white cabbage, shredded
1-1/4 cups Chicken Stock, see page 27
1 tablespoon soy sauce
1 teaspoon chili sauce
4 oz. fine egg noodles

In a wok or deep 10-inch skillet, heat oil. Add garlic and ginger. Cook, stirring constantly, 1 minute. Add spinach and cabbage. Cook, stirring constantly, until vegetables are bright green and almost tender. Stir in stock, soy sauce and chili sauce. Stir in noodles. Simmer a few minutes until noodles are tender. Makes 4 servings.

Note: Serve as an accompaniment to a meat or chicken dish.

Chicken Sukiyaki

4 oz. rice vermicelli
2 tablespoons vegetable oil
1 onion, finely chopped
1 leek, thinly sliced
1 lb. boneless skinned chicken breasts,
  cut into strips
8 oz. tofu, drained, cut in cubes
2 cups sliced mushrooms (4 oz.)
1 cup Chicken Stock, see page 27
1/4 cup soy sauce
1 tablespoon sugar
Lotus root slices, if desired
Fresh cilantro, if desired

Put vermicelli in a medium-size bowl. Cover with boiling water. Soak 10 minutes. Drain thoroughly. In a deep 10-inch skillet, heat oil. Add onion and leek; cook over medium heat a few minutes or until beginning to soften. Add chicken; cook, stirring, until lightly browned. Stir in mushrooms and tofu. In a small bowl, mix together stock, soy sauce and sugar. Pour into skillet. Simmer gently 10 to 15 minutes or until chicken and vegetables are cooked. Stir in drained vermicelli. Heat through. Garnish with lotus root slices and cilantro, if desired. Makes 4 servings.

Note: Sukiyaki refers to the method of cooking at the table in a large heavy pan. Diners help themselves to the cooked meat and vegetables, dipping them in beaten egg before eating them.

Spicy Sesame Noodles

2 tablespoons sesame seeds
1 tablespoon sesame oil
4 teaspoons peanut butter
2 tablespoon soy sauce
2 teaspoons chili sauce
1/2 teaspoon sugar
1/4 cup water
8 oz. rice vermicelli
Carrot blossoms, if desired
Toasted sesame seeds, if desired

In a 6-inch skillet, brown sesame seeds over medium heat. Crush slightly. In a bowl or food processor, mix together browned sesame seeds, sesame oil, peanut butter, soy sauce, chili sauce, sugar and water. Set aside. Put vermicelli into a medium-size bowl. Cover with boiling water. Soak 10 minutes. Drain thoroughly. Put drained vermicelli and sesame sauce in a 2-1/2-quart saucepan. Mix together to coat vermicelli in sauce. Cook over low heat until thoroughly heated through. Garnish with carrot blossoms and sesame seeds, if desired. Makes 4 servings.

Singapore Noodles

2 tablespoons vegetable oil
2 cups sliced mushrooms (4 oz.)
1 onion, finely chopped
1 garlic clove, crushed
4 oz. ham, cut in shreds (1/2 cup)
1 (1-inch) cube ginger root, grated
8 oz. rice vermicelli
1 teaspoon curry powder
Salt
2 cups shredded cooked chicken
4 oz. cooked peeled deveined shrimp
    (3/4 cup)
1/4 cup frozen green peas, thawed
1/3 cup Chicken Stock, see page 27
4 teaspoons soy sauce
1/4 cup dry sherry
Green onion daisies, if desired

In a deep 10-inch skillet, heat vegetable oil. Add mushrooms, onion, garlic, ham and ginger. Stir well. Cook over low heat 15 minutes. Put vermicelli into a bowl. Cover with boiling water. Soak 10 minutes. Drain thoroughly. Stir curry powder and salt into mushroom-ham mixture. Add chicken, shrimp, green peas, stock, soy sauce and sherry; stir thoroughly. Add noodles; stir over low heat until heated through. Garnish with green onion daisies, if desired. Makes 4 servings.

— Buckwheat Noodles with Eggs —

12 oz. buckwheat noodles
2 tablespoons vegetable oil
1 onion, chopped
4 cups shredded Chinese
  cabbage (6 oz.)
4 eggs, beaten
Salt and pepper
1 tablespoon soy sauce
Fresh bay leaf, if desired
Lemon peel rose, if desired

In a large saucepan of boiling salted water, cook noodles in the same way as spaghetti until tender. Drain. Meanwhile, in a large saucepan, heat oil. Add onion; cook until soft. Add Chinese cabbage; cook until beginning to soften. Stir in eggs. Cook, stirring, about 1 minute or until eggs are beginning to set. Stir drained noodles into egg mixture. Add salt, pepper and soy sauce. Garnish with bay leaf and lemon peel rose, if desired, and serve at once. Makes 4 servings.

Vermicelli with Rice & Garbanzo Beans

2/3 cup dried garbanzo beans (chick
  peas), soaked overnight in water
  to cover
1/4 cup butter
1 onion, finely chopped
6 oz. vermicelli
1-1/4 cups long-grain rice
2-1/2 cups water
Salt
1/3 cup sour cream
Fresh Italian parsley, if desired

Drain beans; rinse in cold water. Put into a medium-size saucepan with cold water to cover. Bring to a boil; reduce heat. Cover pan. Cook over low heat 30 minutes or until beans are tender. Meanwhile, in a large saucepan, melt butter. Add onion; cook gently until tender. Break vermicelli into 1-inch pieces. Add to pan. Stir until well-coated with butter. Add rice; cook, stirring, until grains are transparent. Add water and salt to taste. Bring to a boil. Cover pan tightly. Reduce heat to low; simmer about 25 minutes or until water is absorbed and rice is tender. Add more water if needed. Stir beans into vermicelli and rice. Cook over low heat until heated through. Spoon sour cream on top. Garnish with parsley, if desired. Makes 6 servings.

Greek Ravioli

1 egg
2 cups bread flour
1/3 cup water
2 tablespoons butter
1/3 cup grated Parmesan cheese (1 oz.)
Fresh oregano leaves, if desired
Ripe olives, if desired

Filling:
1 cup grated Parmesan cheese
   (about 4 oz.)
3 cups shredded mozzarella cheese or
   Greek Haloumi cheese (12 oz.)
3 egg yolks
Salt, pepper and nutmeg

Make a pasta dough with egg, flour and water, see page 10. Wrap in a damp cloth. Make filling. Roll out pasta dough and fill as for ravioli, see page 16. Preheat oven to 375F

(190C). In a large saucepan of boiling salted water, cook ravioli 10 to 15 minutes or until tender but firm. Drain; arrange in a greased baking dish. Dot with butter; sprinkle with 1/3 cup Parmesan cheese. Bake 10 to 15 minutes or until brown. Garnish with oregano leaves and olives, if desired. Makes 6 servings.

To make filling: In a blender or food processor, process Parmesan cheese, mozzarella cheese and egg yolks to form a smooth paste. Season with salt, pepper and nutmeg.

Variation
Prepare ravioli from Tomato Pasta, see page 11, in half-moon shapes, see page 17.

— Baked Spaghetti & Eggplant —

2 medium-size eggplants, sliced
Salt
Olive oil
1 lb. spaghetti, cooked
1 recipe Tomato Sauce, see page 45
3 hard-cooked eggs, thinly sliced
3/4 cup grated Parmesan
  cheese (2-1/4 oz.)
Chopped hard-cooked egg, if desired

Arrange sliced eggplants in a colander. Sprinkle with salt; drain at least 30 minutes. Preheat oven to 375F (190C). Remove eggplant slices from colander and pat dry. In a large skillet, heat 2 tablespoons olive oil. Fry eggplant in batches until very tender, adding more oil as necessary. Drain on paper towels. In a large bowl, mix together spaghetti and Tomato Sauce. Spread a third of spaghetti mixture in a greased 4-quart oblong baking dish. Cover with half of eggplant slices and half of egg slices. Sprinkle with a third of Parmesan cheese. Repeat layers, finishing with a layer of spaghetti. Sprinkle with remaining Parmesan cheese. Bake 30 minutes or until golden. Garnish with chopped egg, if desired. Makes 6 servings.

—— Japanese Curried Noodles ——

2 tablespoons vegetable oil
1 onion, chopped
1 garlic clove, crushed
1 potato, cut in 1/2-inch cubes
1 carrot, cut in matchsticks
1/2 small red bell pepper, cut
  in small dice
8 oz. boneless skinned chicken
  breasts, cut in small cubes
1-1/2 teaspoons curry powder
1 (1-inch) cube fresh ginger
  root, grated
2/3 cup water
Salt
3-1/2 cups noodles (6 oz.), cooked
2 tablespoons finely chopped
  green onions
Green onion daisy, if desired

In a large saucepan, heat oil. Add onion and garlic; cook over low heat until tender. Add potato, carrot, bell pepper and chicken to pan. Cook over medium heat, stirring occcasionally, until chicken begins to brown. Stir in curry powder, ginger and water. Season with salt. Cover pan; reduce heat to low and cook, stirring occasionally, until vegetables are tender and sauce has thickened. Stir noodles into chicken mixture. Cook a few minutes over medium heat until heated through. Serve in individual bowls. Garnish with green onions and green onion daisy, if desired. Makes 4 servings.

Moroccan Macaroni Pie

4 teaspoons vegetable oil
1 onion, finely chopped
1 garlic clove, crushed
12 oz. boneless shoulder of lamb, cut
   in 1-inch cubes
1 (15-oz.) can tomatoes, drained,
   chopped
2 tablespoons tomato paste
1/2 teaspoon ground cinnamon
1/2 teaspoon ground cumin
Salt and pepper
2-1/2 cups macaroni (12 oz.), cooked
8 sheets filo pastry
1/4 cup butter, melted
Fresh cilantro, if desired

In a medium-size saucepan, heat oil. Add onion and garlic. Cook over medium heat until soft. Add lamb to onion; stir until brown. Stir in tomatoes, tomato paste, cinnamon and cumin. Season with salt and pepper. Cover pan; reduce heat to low. Cook 1-1/2 hours or until lamb is tender and sauce is thick. Stir in macaroni. Heat oven to 425F (220C). Line a 3-quart oblong baking dish with a sheet of filo pastry, leaving edges overhanging dish. Brush pastry with melted butter. Repeat with 3 more sheets of pastry and butter. Fill dish with macaroni mixture. Top with 4 more sheets of pastry, brushing each with melted butter. Tuck edges of pastry down inside dish. Brush top with melted butter. Bake 15 minutes. Reduce oven temperature to 325F (160C). Bake 30 minutes longer or until pastry is cooked and top is crisp. Garnish with cilantro, if desired. Makes 4 to 6 servings.

Crabmeat & Noodles

8 oz. egg noodles
2 tablespoons vegetable oil
1 cup fresh or frozen crabmeat,
   thawed
8 oz. Chinese cabbage, coarsely
   shredded (5 cups)
4 teaspoons chili bean sauce
2 teaspoons soy sauce
1 cup light chicken stock
2 green onions, finely chopped

In a large saucepan of boiling salted
water, cook noodles until just tender
to the bite. Drain thoroughly. Pour
into a hot serving dish. Keep warm.
In a wok or deep 10-inch skillet, heat
oil. Stir-fry crabmeat and Chinese
cabbage 2 minutes. Add chili bean
sauce, soy sauce and stock. Cook 2 to
3 minutes, stirring. Pour sauce over
noodles. Garnish with green onions.
Serve at once. Makes 4 servings.

Chow Mein

8 oz. Chinese egg noodles
6 oz. pork tenderloin, cut in
   julienne strips
1 teaspoon cornstarch
4 teaspoons light soy sauce
2 teaspoons dry sherry
2 tablespoons vegetable oil
2 oz. Chinese pea pods, trimmed
1/2 cucumber, peeled, cut in
   julienne strips
1 tablespoon green onions, finely
   chopped
1 teaspoon sesame oil
Cucumber flower, if desired

Cook noodles according to directions on package. Drain; rinse with cold water. Let drain. In a medium-size bowl, mix together pork, cornstarch, 2 teaspoons of soy sauce and sherry. Marinate 10 minutes. In a wok or skillet, heat 1 tablespoon of vegetable oil. Add drained noodles; stir-fry 2 to 3 minutes. Remove to a heated serving dish; keep warm. Heat remaining 1 tablespoon of vegetable oil in wok or skillet. Add pork, pea pods and cucumber; stir-fry 4 to 5 minutes. Stir in remaining 2 teaspoons of soy sauce. Pour over noodles. Sprinkle with green onions and sesame oil. Garnish with cucumber flower, if desired, and serve. Makes 4 servings.

Fried Won-Ton Skins

2 cups bread flour
1 egg
1/3 cup water
Vegetable oil
Chili flower, if desired
Hot chili sauce

Filling:
4 teaspoons finely chopped
  green onions
1 (1-inch) cube fresh ginger
  root, grated
8 oz. ground pork
1/2 (10-oz.) pkg. frozen chopped
  spinach, cooked
1 tablespoon soy sauce
1 tablespoon dry sherry
1 egg, beaten
1/2 teaspoon cornstarch

Mix together flour, egg and water to make a pasta dough, see page 10. Wrap in a damp cloth. Make filling.

To make won-ton skins, roll out dough, see page 12, in 3-inch squares. Put a teaspoon of filling in middle of each square. Pinch top edges firmly together to seal. In a deep-fat fryer, heat oil to 375F (190C) or until a dry cube of bread turns golden in 50 seconds. Fry won-tons in several batches until brown and crisp. Drain on paper towels. Garnish with chili flower, if desired, and serve at once with hot chili sauce. Makes about 24 fried won-tons.

To make filling: In a medium-size bowl, combine green onions, ginger, pork, spinach, soy sauce, sherry, egg and cornstarch. Mix thoroughly.

Note: You can buy ready-made fresh or frozen won-ton skins from Chinese grocers.

Vegetable Casserole

2 tablespoons vegetable oil
1 onion, thinly sliced
2 teaspoons all-purpose flour
1 tablespoon paprika
1 (15-oz.) can tomatoes
Water
3 cups cauliflowerets
2 carrots, coarsely chopped
1/2 green bell pepper, coarsely
  chopped
2 medium zucchini, cut in thick
  diagonal slices
2 cups whole-wheat pasta shells (4 oz.)
Salt and pepper
2/3 cup plain yogurt
Fresh Italian parsley, if desired

In a saucepan, heat oil. Add onion;
cook until soft. Stir in flour and paprika. Cook, stirring, 1 minute. Add
tomatoes with juice and water. Bring
to a boil. Stir in cauliflowerets, carrots, bell pepper, zucchini and pasta.
Season with salt and pepper. Cover
pan; simmer 40 minutes or until pasta is tender. Gently stir yogurt into
vegetable mixture. Garnish with
parsley, if desired. Makes 4 servings.

— Macaroni & Vegetable Bake —

1 cup thinly sliced leeks
2 celery stalks
1 red bell pepper
3/4 cup whole-wheat macaroni (4 oz.),
 cooked
2/3 cup plain yogurt
1 cup low-fat soft cheese (4 oz.)
Salt and pepper
2 teaspoons soy sauce
1/2 cup shredded Cheddar
 cheese (2 oz.)

Preheat oven to 350F (175C). Put leeks into a saucepan of boiling water. Bring back to a boil. Drain. Finely chop celery and bell pepper. In a medium-size bowl, mix together leeks, celery, bell pepper and macaroni. In another bowl, mix together yogurt, soft cheese, salt, pepper and soy sauce. Pour over macaroni mixture. Mix together thoroughly. Put into an ovenproof dish; cover with Cheddar cheese. Bake 30 minutes or until golden and bubbling. Makes 4 servings.

— Vegetarian Bolognese Sauce —

2-3/4 cups water
1 cup lentils (6 oz.)
2/3 cup split peas (4 oz.)
2 tablespoons vegetable oil
1 onion, finely chopped
1 garlic clove, crushed
1 carrot, finely chopped
1 celery stalk, finely chopped
1 (15-oz.) can tomatoes, drained, chopped
1 teaspoon dried leaf oregano
Salt and pepper

In a medium-size saucepan, bring water to a boil. Stir in lentils and split peas. Simmer, covered, about 40 minutes or until all liquid has been absorbed and lentils and peas are soft. In a medium-size saucepan, heat oil. Add onion, garlic, carrot and celery. Cook over low heat, stirring occasionally, until soft. Stir in tomatoes and oregano. Season with salt and pepper. Cover pan; simmer gently 5 minutes. Add cooked lentils and split peas to vegetable mixture. Cook, stirring occasionally, until well combined and heated through. Makes 4 to 6 servings.

Note: Serve with whole-wheat spaghetti, if desired.

Pasta & Vegetable Loaf

2-1/2 cups water
2/3 cup lentils (4 oz.)
2/3 cup split peas (4 oz.)
1/4 cup butter
1 onion, chopped
1 garlic clove, crushed
1 large carrot, chopped
1 celery stalk, chopped
2 cups small whole-wheat pasta
   shapes (4 oz.), cooked
1 egg, beaten
1/2 teaspoon ground cumin
2 tablespoons chopped fresh parsley
Salt and pepper

In a medium-size saucepan, bring water to a boil. Stir in lentils and split peas. Simmer, covered, about 40 minutes or until all liquid has been absorbed and lentils and peas are soft. Preheat oven to 375F (190C). In a saucepan, heat butter. Add onion, garlic, carrot and celery. Cook, stirring occasionally, until soft. Add cooked lentils and split peas, pasta, egg, cumin and parsley. Season with salt and pepper. Mix together thoroughly. Spoon mixture into a greased 9" x 5" loaf pan. Cover top with foil. Bake 40 minutes. Let stand in pan 5 minutes. Run a knife around edge of loaf and turn out onto a serving dish. Makes 4 servings.

Note: This loaf may be served hot with tomato sauce or cold with salad.

Vegetarian Lasagne

1 cup adzuki beans (6 oz.), soaked
   overnight
4 cups cold water
6 to 8 whole-wheat lasagne noodles
2 tablespoons vegetable oil
1 onion, finely chopped
1 garlic clove, crushed
8 oz. white cabbage, coarsely
   shredded (4 cups)
2 cups sliced mushrooms (4 oz.)
1 leek, coarsely chopped
1/2 green bell pepper,
   coarsely chopped
1 (15-oz.) can tomatoes
1 teaspoon dried leaf oregano
Salt and pepper
1 recipe Béchamel Sauce, see page 48,
   made with whole-wheat flour
1/2 cup shredded Cheddar
   cheese (2 oz.)
Fresh tarragon, if desired

Drain adzuki beans. Put into a sauce-pan with cold water. Bring to a boil. Cover pan; reduce heat. Simmer 40 minutes or until tender. Cook noodles, see pages 7-8. Drain; lay on paper towels. In a large saucepan, heat oil. Add onion and garlic. Cook until soft. Stir in cabbage, mushrooms, leek and bell pepper. Cook 5 minutes, stirring occasionally. Drain adzuki beans, reserving cooking liquid. Add beans to vegetables. Stir in tomatoes with juice and 1 cup of cooking liquid from beans. Add oregano. Season with salt and pepper. Cover pan; simmer gently 30 minutes, stirring occasionally. Preheat oven to 350F (175C). In a greased baking dish, layer noodles, vegetables and Béchamel sauce, ending with a layer of sauce. Sprinkle cheese over top. Bake 30 minutes or until golden and bubbling. Garnish with tarragon, if desired. Makes 4 to 6 servings.

Note: Serve with a carrot salad.

Pasta Pan Fry

2 tablespoons vegetable oil
1 onion, chopped
1 green bell pepper, chopped
2 cups sliced mushrooms (4 oz.)
8 oz. chicken livers, chopped (1 cup)
8 oz. tomatoes, peeled, chopped
Salt and pepper
2 fresh sage leaves, chopped
4 cups pasta bows (8 oz.), cooked
Additional fresh sage leaves, if desired

In a large skillet, heat oil. Add onion
and bell pepper; cook, stirring occasionally, 5 minutes or until soft. Add
mushrooms. Cook, stirring, 2 minutes. Add chicken livers. Cook, stirring, until livers are no longer pink.
Stir in tomatoes, salt, pepper and
chopped sage leaves. Cook, stirring,
until the juice begins to run from
tomatoes. Add pasta bows; cook for a
few minutes until heated through.
Garnish with additional sage leaves, if
desired. Makes 4 servings.

—— Golden Macaroni Fritters ——

1/2 cup macaroni (2 oz.)
2 eggs
1 cup shredded Cheddar cheese (4 oz.)
2/3 cup canned whole-kernel corn,
    drained
Salt and pepper
Vegetable oil for deep-frying
Italian parsley, if desired

Cook macaroni in boiling salted
water until just tender to the bite.
Drain and rinse with cold water. In a
medium-size bowl, beat eggs; add
cooked macaroni, cheese and corn.
Season with salt and pepper. Stir
thoroughly. In a deep skillet, heat oil
to 375F (190C). Drop tablespoonfuls
of macaroni mixture into hot oil. Fry
until each fritter is crisp and golden
on underside and upper side is set.
Turn and fry until other side is crisp
and golden. Drain on paper towels.
Garnish with parsley, if desired, and
serve. Makes 4 servings.

Deep-Fried Ravioli

1 (10-oz.) pkg. frozen chopped
  spinach, cooked, drained
1-1/3 cups chopped cooked chicken
2 egg yolks
1/3 cup grated Parmesan cheese (1 oz.)
Salt, pepper and nutmeg
Fresh Pasta, using 3 eggs, see page 10
Vegetable oil for deep-frying
Lemon and lime slices, if desired
Fresh parsley, if desired

Squeeze as much water as possible
from spinach. In a blender or food
processor, process spinach, chicken,
egg yolks and Parmesan cheese until
quite smooth. Season with salt, pepper and nutmeg. Roll out pasta
dough, see page 12. Using chicken
mixture as a filling, make ravioli, see
page 16. In a deep fryer, heat oil to
375F (190C) or until a 1-inch bread
cube turns golden in 40 seconds. Fry
ravioli in batches until crisp and gold-
en brown. Drain on paper towels.
Garnish with lemon and lime slices
and parsley, if desired, and serve.
Makes 4 servings.

Pizza-Style Spaghettini

8 oz. spaghettini
1 cup shredded Cheddar cheese (4 oz.)
2 eggs, beaten
4 oz. salami, diced (2/3 cup)
1/2 teaspoon dried leaf oregano
Salt and pepper
2 tablespoons vegetable oil
2 tomatoes, sliced
6 ripe olives
Fresh oregano, if desired

Cook spaghettini, see pages 7-8.
Drain; rinse with cold water. In a
large bowl, using hands, mix together
spaghettini, cheese, eggs, salami and
dried oregano. Season with salt and
pepper. In a medium-size skillet, heat
oil. Spoon spaghettini mixture into
pan; pat out evenly. Cook about 5
minutes or until underside is brown
and crisp and top is set. Turn over
onto a plate; slide back into pan.
Cook second side until brown and
crisp. Turn out onto a large serving
plate. Garnish with tomato slices,
olives and fresh oregano, if desired.
Makes 4 to 6 servings.

Crispy Cannelloni

8 cannelloni tubes
2 tablespoons vegetable oil
1 leek, finely chopped
8 oz. low-fat soft cheese
4 oz. mortadella, chopped
1 teaspoon tomato paste
2 eggs
1 tablespoon chopped fresh parsley
Salt and pepper
1/3 cup fresh bread crumbs
1/3 cup grated Parmesan cheese (1 oz.)
Vegetable oil for deep-frying
Lemon slices, if desired, cut in half
Fresh parsley, if desired

In a large pan of boiling salted water, cook cannelloni 4 to 5 minutes or until almost soft. Drain, rinse with cold water and spread out on paper towels. In a small skillet, heat oil. Add leek; sauté until soft. In a medium-size bowl, mix together leek, soft cheese, mortadella, tomato paste, 1 of the eggs, parsley, salt and pepper. Using a teaspoon, push filling into cannelloni. Mix together bread crumbs and Parmesan cheese. Spread out on a large plate. Beat remaining egg in a flat bowl. Roll cannelloni in beaten egg and coat with bread crumb mixture. In a deep fryer, heat oil to 375F (190C) or until a 1-inch bread cube turns golden in 40 seconds. Fry cannelloni, 4 at a time, 2 to 3 minutes or until crisp and golden. Drain on paper towels. Keep hot while frying remaining cannelloni. Garnish with lemon slices and parsley, if desired. Makes 4 servings.

—— Crispy Noodles & Onions ——

**1-2/3 cups short cut noodles
    (6 oz.), cooked
Vegetable oil for deep-frying
1 large Spanish onion,
    thinly sliced
1/3 cup milk
2 tablespoons all-purpose flour
Salt
Green onion daisy, if desired
Lemon butterfly, if desired**

In a deep fryer, heat oil to 375F
(190C) or until a 1-inch bread cube
turns golden in 40 seconds. Fry noodles in 4 batches until crisp and gold-
en. Drain on paper towels. Keep hot.
Separate onion slices in rings. Dip onion rings into milk; toss in flour. Fry
onion rings in 2 batches until crisp
and golden. Mix with noodles;
sprinkle with salt. Garnish with green
onion daisy and lemon butterfly, if
desired, and serve at once. Makes 4
servings as an accompaniment.

Variation
Substitute green noodles for part of
plain noodles.

Noodle Pancakes

1 oz. noodles, cooked
2 (1-oz.) thin ham slices
2 eggs, beaten
1 tablespoon chopped fresh parsley
1 tablespoon grated Parmesan cheese,
Salt and pepper
Vegetable oil for deep-frying
Lemon slices, if desired
Fresh parsley, if desired

Chop noodles and ham. In a medium-size bowl, mix chopped noodles and ham with eggs, parsley and Parmesan cheese. Season with salt and pepper. In a deep skillet, heat oil. Drop tablespoonfuls of noodle mixture into hot oil. Cook until underside is crisp and brown; turn over and fry other side. Remove and drain on paper towels. Garnish with lemon slices and parsley, if desired, and serve at once. Makes 4 servings.

─── Chocolate & Nut Bows ───

3-1/2 cups pasta bows (8 oz.)
1/4 cup blanched almonds
1/4 cup hazelnuts
2 tablespoons butter
2 squares semisweet chocolate,
  coarsely chopped
2 tablespoons light-brown sugar

In a large pan of boiling salted water, cook pasta bows until just tender to the bite. Meanwhile, put nuts in a broiler pan; broil, stirring frequently, until golden brown. Chop nuts coarsely. Drain pasta; put into a warmed serving dish. Stir in butter. Add chopped nuts, chocolate and brown sugar. Toss to mix thoroughly. Serve at once. Makes 4 servings.

Note: Substitute Farfalle (pasta butterflies) for pasta bows, if desired.

Almond Ravioli & Raspberry Sauce

1-1/4 cups ground almonds
1/2 cup powdered sugar
2 egg yolks
2 tablespoons butter
1 recipe Fresh Pasta, see page 10
Plain yogurt
Raspberry leaves, if desired

Raspberry Sauce:
4 cups raspberries
1/2 cup powdered sugar

In a bowl, mix together ground almonds, powdered sugar and egg yolks. In a small saucepan, melt butter. Add to almond mixture. Roll out pasta dough, see page 12. Make ravioli, see page 16, filling with ground almond paste. In a large pan of boiling water, cook ravioli about 10 minutes or until tender but firm; drain. Make sauce. Pour a pool of sauce on 4 dessert plates and arrange ravioli on top. Spoon yogurt into a pastry bag fitted with a plain tip. Pipe a circle of yogurt around each dish. Using a skewer, make a web effect. Decorate with reserved raspberries and raspberry leaves, if desired. Makes 4 servings.

To make sauce: Reserve a few raspberries for decoration. Mix remaining raspberries and sugar in a medium-size saucepan. Heat gently until juice begins to run. Press through a sieve.

Apple Lasagne

1-1/4 cups milk
1 egg
1 egg yolk
1 tablespoon cornstarch
1 tablespoon powdered sugar
1-3/4 lbs. cooking apples
2 tablespoons butter
1/3 cup powdered sugar
Water
1/4 cup raisins
1/2 teaspoon apple pie spice
6 lasagne noodles
1/4 cup walnuts, finely chopped
Powdered sugar, if desired
Whipped cream, if desired

In a medium-size saucepan, heat milk. In a medium-size bowl, mix together egg, egg yolk, cornstarch and 1 tablespoon powdered sugar.

Pour hot milk into egg mixture while stirring. Return to saucepan; cook over medium low heat, stirring constantly, until thickened. Set aside. Peel, core and slice apples. Put into a medium-size saucepan with butter, 1/3 cup powdered sugar and a little water. Cook 10 minutes or until apples are soft. Stir in raisins and apple pie spice. Preheat oven to 375F (190C). In a large pan of boiling water, cook noodles, see pages 7-8; drain. In a buttered baking dish, layer lasagne and apple mixture, ending with an apple layer. Pour custard over apples. Sprinkle with walnuts. Bake 25 minutes or until set. Decorate with powdered sugar and serve with a dollop of whipped cream, if desired. Makes 4 servings.

Indian Milk Pudding

2 tablespoons butter
2 oz. spaghetti, broken into 1-inch
  pieces
3-3/4 cups milk
4 cardamon pods, crushed
2 tablespoons golden raisins
1/4 cup slivered almonds
1/4 cup powdered sugar
Silver leaves, if desired

In a heavy saucepan, melt butter.
Add spaghetti; cook, stirring, until
spaghetti begins to brown. Add milk,
cardamon pods, raisins and almonds.
Simmer about 20 minutes or until
spaghetti is tender, stirring frequently. Add sugar; cook 5 more minutes.
Let cool, stirring occasionally. Pour
into a serving dish; cover. Refrigerate
overnight. Decorate with silver
leaves, if desired, and serve cold.
Makes 4 servings.

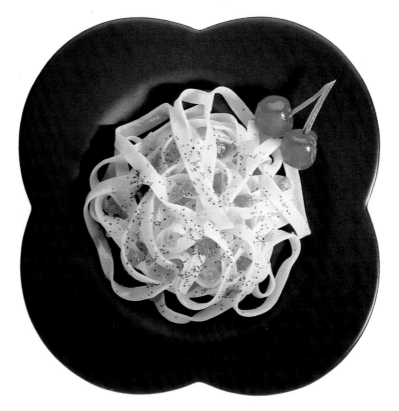

Polish Noodles

8 oz. tagliatelle
3 tablespoons poppy seeds
2 tablespoons butter
2 tablespoons honey
1/3 cup candied cherries, chopped
2 tablespoons chopped mixed peel
Glacé cherries, if desired
Angelica, if desired

In a large pan of boiling water, cook tagliatelle until just tender to the bite. Drain well. Heat poppy seeds in a skillet over medium heat 1 minute, shaking pan occasionally. In a saucepan, melt butter. Add honey, cherries and mixed peel. Pour tagliatelle into a warmed serving dish. Add honey mixture. Mix together well. Decorate with glacé cherries and angelica, if desired. Makes 4 servings.

——— Apricot & Walnut Layer ———

1 cup dried apricots, soaked overnight
  in water to cover (or cover with
  boiling water; let stand 3 minutes)
1 (1-inch) piece cinnamon stick
Juice and grated peel of 1 orange
1/2 cup packed brown sugar
2 teaspoons cornstarch
Water
1/4 cup butter
1/2 cup fine fresh bread crumbs
4 oz. tagliatelle, cooked
1/2 cup ground walnuts
Walnut halves, if desired
Additional apricot pieces, if desired
Orange-flavored sour cream, if desired

Drain apricots, reserving liquid. Put
apricots, 2 tablespoons of apricot liquid, cinnamon, orange juice and
peel and 2 tablespoons of brown
sugar into a medium-size saucepan.
Bring to a boil; reduce heat. Simmer,
covered, 10 to 15 minutes or until
apricots are tender. Blend cornstarch
with a little water. Add to apricots.
Cook gently, stirring constantly, until
mixture has thickened. Cool. Preheat
oven to 375F (190C). Butter a soufflé
dish with 2 tablespoons of butter;
coat with bread crumbs. Put a third of
pasta into dish. Cover with apricot
mixture. Cover with half of remaining pasta. Mix together ground walnuts and remaining brown sugar;
spread over pasta. Top with remaining pasta. In a saucepan, melt
remaining 2 tablespoons of butter.
Pour over pasta. Bake in oven 25
minutes. Turn out onto a serving
dish. Garnish with walnut halves and
additional apricot pieces, if desired.
Serve with sour cream, if desired.
Makes 4 to 6 servings.

—— Date & Noodle Pudding ——

2/3 cup plain yogurt
1/2 cup mascarpone (4 oz.)
1 teaspoon cornstarch
3 eggs, beaten
2 tablespoons honey
1 teaspoon ground cinnamon
1/3 cup chopped dates
1/3 cup golden raisins
1/3 cup candied cherries, chopped
8 oz. tagliatelle, cooked
Whipped cream, if desired
Glacé cherries, if desired

Preheat oven to 350F (175C). In a medium-size bowl, mix together yogurt, mascarpone, cornstarch, eggs, honey, cinnamon, dates, raisins and candied cherries. Add tagliatelle to fruit mixture. Stir well to distribute fruit evenly. Spoon into a greased round baking dish. Level the surface. Bake about 40 minutes or until set and golden brown. Serve warm or cold, decorated with whipped cream and glacé cherries, if desired. Makes 4 servings.

—— Pear & Pasta Pudding ——

2/3 cup macaroni (3 oz.)
2 cups milk
2 pears
1/3 cup raisins
Grated peel of 1 lemon
1/2 teaspoon ground cinnamon
1 tablespoon brown sugar
1 egg, separated
3 tablespoons butter

Preheat oven to 350F (175C). Put macaroni and milk in a saucepan. Bring to a boil; reduce heat. Simmer 10 minutes or until macaroni is tender and milk is absorbed. Remove from heat. Peel and core 1 pear. Chop coarsely; add to macaroni with raisins, lemon peel, cinnamon, brown sugar and egg yolk. In a small bowl, whisk egg white until stiff. Gently fold into macaroni mixture. Pour into a greased baking dish. Bake 30 minutes. Peel and core remaining pear. Cut into slices lengthwise. Arrange decoratively around edge of pudding. In a saucepan, melt butter. Brush over pears. Return to the oven for 10 minutes or until pear slices are brown. Makes 4 servings.

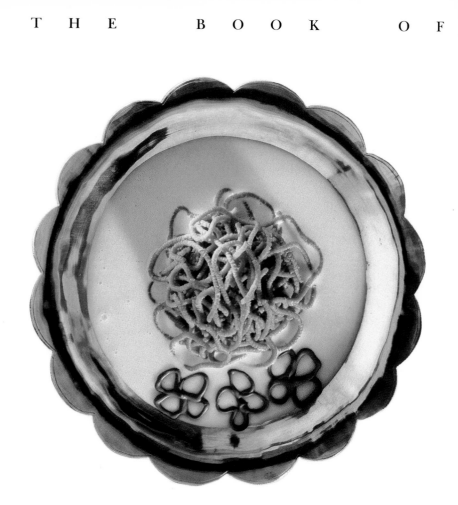

Chocolate Spaghetti & White Chocolate Sauce

**2 oz. semisweet chocolate, melted,
  cooled**
2 eggs
1-3/4 cups bread flour
Chocolate rosettes, if desired

White Chocolate Sauce:
2 oz. white chocolate
2/3 cup whipping cream

Add melted chocolate to eggs. Make pasta, page 10, using chocolate-egg mixture and bread flour. Let rest 30 minutes. Roll out pasta. Roll pasta sheets through a spaghetti cutter. Put a towel over back of a chair. Spread spaghetti out; let dry 30 minutes. In a large pan of boiling water, cook spaghetti until just tender to the bite. Drain spaghetti. Make sauce. Serve spaghetti with sauce. Garnish with chocolate rosettes, if desired. Makes 4 servings.

To make sauce: Put white chocolate and cream into a saucepan over low heat. Cook, stirring constantly, until chocolate is melted and smooth.

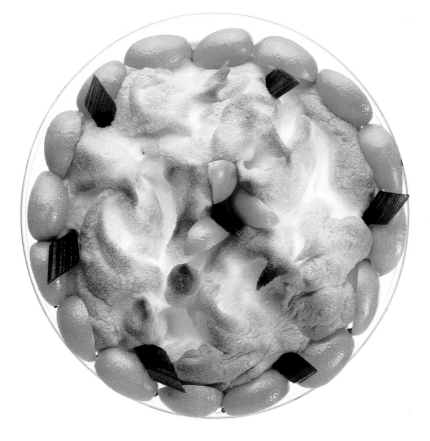

—— Pasta Meringue Pudding ——

3/4 cup ditalina (4 oz.)
About 1-3/4 cups milk
1/3 cup powdered sugar
Grated peel of 1 orange
2 eggs, separated
2 tablespoons butter
Kumquat segments, if desired
Angelica leaves, if desired

Put ditalina and 1-3/4 cups milk into a medium-size saucepan. Bring to a boil; reduce heat. Simmer gently 20 minutes or until pasta is tender and milk has been absorbed, adding more milk if necessary. Preheat oven to 300F (150C). Add 5 teaspoons of powdered sugar, orange peel and egg yolks to pasta. Stir well. In a small saucepan, melt butter. Add to pasta mixture. Pour into a greased baking dish. In a bowl, whisk egg whites until stiff. Whisk in all but 1 teaspoon of remaining powdered sugar. Spoon or pipe meringue over pasta mixture. Sprinkle with remaining 1 teaspoon of powdered sugar. Bake 30 minutes or until golden brown and crisp. Decorate with kumquat sections and angelica leaves, if desired. Makes 4 servings.

INDEX

PRINTED IN BELGIUM BY
proost
INTERNATIONAL BOOK PRODUCTION